Cry Purple

One Woman's Journey through Homelessness, Crack Addiction and Prison to Blindness, Motherhood and Happiness

Christine McDonald

Copyright 2013 by Christine McDonald

All rights reserved.

ISBN: 1482053616
ISBN-13: 978-1482053616

DEDICATION

For Ricky, the light of my life,
and for Mary Christine,
whom I loved enough to give up for adoption

Table of Contents

Preface

My Early Life and Self–Image

This is my first attempt at writing a book. I'm inviting you, my readers, to follow along as I recount my journey of life on the streets and what came after that. You'll read how I got into that situation, my life for almost two decades as a homeless street corner prostitute addicted to crack cocaine, and then some details of the far better life I lead now.

I grew up in a little town called Wayne, Oklahoma. Prior to our living there, we had moved a lot and I had changed schools a number of times.

I remember very well the difficulties of changing schools and attempting to make friends, which was something I was not good at. I wore glasses, and back then, glasses always earned taunts such as "Four eyes!" and "Bottle caps!" I had flattened facial features that often got me called "pancake face." I remember walking down a hallway one day at school and being called "Madame Medusa" by my schoolmates. All the kids were covering their eyes, walking along the hallway close to the walls, so as not to touch or look at me. They were all chattering, "If you look at her, you'll turn to stone!" For a long time, this was my daily hallway experience. I always looked down, not daring to make eye contact with my classmates. Every day as a child, I dreaded, if not hated, showing up at school.

These things intimidated me a great deal. They kept me from being able to raise my hand in class to ask questions, as I didn't dare to draw any more attention to myself. I didn't want to risk getting ridiculed in the classroom, as it was hard enough at recess.

In addition to all of the above, I had problems with my joints. Some of my joints were extremely hyper–extendable, meaning I could do things resembling circus tricks with my hands, elbows, and fingers, making me a freak of sorts. However, my hips, knees, and spine were extremely stiff, much less flexible than normal, which kept me from being able to run fast. I always came in last in PE, no matter how hard I tried. I would try and try, hoping to at least come in next to last, even once, but it was no good. My body had such limitations that I couldn't do any tumbling moves or do a simple cartwheel, either.

Outside in our yard at home, I would practice running back and forth the entire length of the yard, working and working to build up speed. I would run and run, also spending hours going up and down stairs, trying desperately to increase my speed and strength. It was only much later in life, when I was in my late thirties, that I learned that none of this was my fault, that I had something known as Stickler syndrome.

On top of everything else, my mom told me I was mentally retarded. I need to emphasize here that I mean no insult to anyone by using that term. It was the common term back then for people with IQs that were lower than average, and it was what my mother called me. So that's why I use the term here.

Although she waited to inform me of this until I was in fourth or fifth grade, this also impacted my self–esteem, adding to the already awkward school experiences I was suffering. Once she had called me that, from that point on, I didn't even try in school. In my own mind, once I took on that label, then I felt that I couldn't learn anything, anyway, so why even try?

Even though my school years were generally so painful, there were a few bright spots. I loved music class and excelled at playing instruments. I was often selected to represent our school by playing at scholastic meets and gatherings of various sorts.

However, I would often skip other classes during the day, choosing instead to walk through open fields, savoring the smell of freshly sun–baked hay or skipping stones across the water. I always felt safe alone, and loved being alone in empty fields.

When I was growing up, my home life was dysfunctional. However, I'm not going to talk about all that here, out of respect for my family and their feelings. I want to emphasize that this book is about me, about my own mistakes and my efforts to correct them. It's about my years of addiction and my journey beyond it. I don't want to make my early home life a focal point of any part of my book.

When I was young, Wayne had a population sign, reading 491, on the outskirts of town. We were miles from even a grocery store. I remember that when I was outside at night, the flat landscape allowed me to see lights for miles. I remember the night skies. The stars were ever so bright, twinkling, gleaming against the blackest of black, endless backgrounds.

After I ran away from home and got on drugs, never in all the cities I ever hitchhiked to, never on any of the streets I worked, have I experienced again the clean, sweet smell of the air back in Wayne. Nor have I ever again seen skies that blue, so crystal clear, with the most beautiful white, fluffy clouds drifting across the sky. Those endless day and night skies were wonderful, amazing things that I've never seen anywhere else.

Another thing I'd like to add is that since those days in Wayne, I've lived in large cities where crime is the daily norm. It seems that someone is killed just about every day in most large U.S. cities. But that was certainly not the case in little Wayne, Oklahoma. So maybe, just maybe, although many things there were quite unpleasant for me, a little piece of me will always be there.

I'm not sure at what age I started to self–mutilate, to cut

myself, often wondering why no one seemed to notice. I think I just wanted someone, anyone, to ask me, "What's wrong?" If that had ever happened, maybe I could have let out some of the emotional turmoil I had pent up inside. But at the same time, I always cut myself in places I could hide. Somehow, the cutting provided me some emotional relief.

Once I started using drugs, I didn't have the need for cutting any longer. Alcohol and drugs were ways that I could self–medicate, helping me to end my emotions, my feelings, my thoughts. I would sneak beer or any other alcoholic drink I could find in the house. I would steal sleeping pills from the medicine cabinet, and when I got home from school, I would take one in order to fall asleep, so I wouldn't have to think about the painful experience of attending school.

However, it was just as painful, if not more so, for me to be at home. It was as if a deep, dark cloud hung over our house, and it hit me whenever I walked in the front door. I won't go into all that, though. Maybe I'll save it for another book.

Perhaps I was broken, somehow, at birth, as I don't remember any years in school that weren't painful for me. I would watch others laugh in school, see all the normal people, the pretty people, the smart people. That's how I viewed everyone around me, seeing them all as prettier than me, as smarter than me. I was retarded, I thought, and I knew that couldn't be changed. So I believed that "pretty" and "smart" were terms that would never apply to me.

I would get grades like "D minus minus." Now who gets grades of D minus minus? Applying my own reason to this, I figured that it was a small town, and they knew I was retarded, so they simply let me pass classes, figuring that I would never be able to learn even if they kept me back, to repeat grades.

As I got into my teen years, my facial features grew and changed, and I no longer had a pancake face. I got contacts, and PE was no longer mandatory, thank God! But by that time, when my classmates would speak to me, it was too painful for me to respond. I had been too scared by all my prior years in school.

I itched to get away from those kids, from all the mean words I remembered from my time in elementary school. It didn't seem possible for me to move beyond all that emotionally, so my obsession was to run away, to find people who hadn't known me as a kid. I just wanted to start over somehow. For once in my awkward life, I wanted to feel pretty and accepted. And I couldn't stand being at home a moment longer.

Maybe that was part of what drew me to dancing in clubs, to stripping, and then to prostitution: not only the drugs, but also knowing that a guy was choosing me, paying me for my looks, my smile. For me, at last, that was acceptance.

Then when I was in my late thirties and newly blind, I learned that I was certainly not retarded, that I had never been. In fact, they told me I had an above-average IQ and could have excelled at anything. I also learned that I had an above-average business aptitude. I was so thrilled to learn that I *did* have the ability to learn, that I was smart enough to do anything and be anything I desired.

So when I was young, was my self-esteem so low that it limited my ability to learn? When I was told that I was retarded, did that make me simply detach from thinking I was able to learn? Who knows? But at last I learned that I was smart, charming, and likable, and that I had an above-average ability to learn. Thus, once I got clean and off drugs, I thrived, soaking up information, loving college in a traditional setting.

During my time on the streets in addiction, I was in a drug-induced haze all the time. Thus my emotions, my education, and my internal growth simply stopped. And once all that was behind me, it soon became clear to me that I had a lot of catching up to do.

But now it's time to get started with this story.

Chapter 1

Introduction to Prostitution and My Life on the Streets

If you're anticipating reading about some specific and gritty incidents from my life as a drug-addicted prostitute, I can assure you that you'll find plenty of those later in the book. But for right now, I want to share a little about prostitution in general — at least about my life as a street corner prostitute and how it all started for me.

Prostitution is the oldest profession in the world. Look at Rahab, in the Bible. Jesus hung out with prostitutes. Prostitution is something that has been in existence since the beginning of civilization, and it will always continue.

I'm going to tell you about my first experience as a prostitute, although at the time I didn't see it as that. I do know that what planted the seed for me was finding out that a pretty smile can help you get what you want.

I was what's known as a "chronic runaway." I first ran away from home at around age 13, but it wasn't until I was 15 that I figured out how not to get caught. Yes, my childhood was rather dysfunctional, but this book is about me and my own mistakes, so I won't take you through all of that.

Who ever plans on a life of prostitution? I certainly hadn't, but after living for a while in an abandoned house without running water or electricity, I was tired, cold, and hungry. One afternoon a man pulled up beside me in his car as I was walking down the street with no destination. He asked if I needed a ride. I was cold. I could feel the warmth from the inside of his car, so I said, "Sure."

He bought me food from Sonic and put me in a hotel room. It was a beautiful room, clean and cozy, with pretty, colorful blankets. I had never been in a hotel like that, and I even got to experience pizza delivery for the first time. Today I know the hotel was a La Quinta Inn, so it was no Ritz Carlton, but to me, it was super fancy.

He bought me ice cream and candy and soda, and he offered to take my clothes to be washed. They smelled and were blackened with dirt. There in the hotel, given that I had just taken a hot shower and had washed my hair, the mere thought of putting those clothes on again turned my stomach, so I agreed.

I had dabbled with drugs by this time, drinking and popping pills. I would steal booze from my folks and take any and all pills that I could get my hands on, whatever would put me to sleep. It was my escape. What I couldn't find at home, I would get from classmates. There was no cocaine in my life as yet.

When I let that man pick me up and take me to that hotel, it was about survival, not addiction. He bought me security and supplied my basic needs, if just for a brief time. He said I was pretty. We didn't have sex. He asked if he could take a couple of nude photos of me, telling me how beautiful I was. I surely didn't feel beautiful, and I hadn't even before then, so what he was telling me was very flattering. Afterwards, he left me in the room, left me money on the desk by the TV set, and I never saw him again.

I didn't become a street corner hooker from that one experience. It was just the first experience I had of being paid for nothing more than being a pretty young girl, at least in the eyes of that one guy.

After that experience, I returned to my little abandoned house with my mattress on a floor in a room. A few days later, walking again with no direction, I was picked up by a guy who sold roses and other flowers in bars. He made me a fake ID. He bought me a couple of pretty dresses and would drop me off at night clubs. I would smile, engage in a little small talk, sell flowers, and get tips, and I was paid cash at the end of each night. Soon I had it down. Like an actress on a stage, I learned to smile and tell the guys what they wanted to hear. Then the sales and the tips were on. The tips got bigger as I got better at my act. This was not prostitution, but I was learning that it was possible to make money just by smiling cutely and making small talk. I was learning that this was a way to take care of my needs.

Later, I moved on to being a stripper in a club, drinking and being tipped drugs, like pills and cocaine. That was the tipping point for me.

Being on stage felt like being somebody. When the same guys would return just to see me dance, I felt special. After work, sometimes I would just hang out with the girls, and sometimes I would get asked out by the men who came to the club to watch me dance. They bought me nice dinners and took me to nice hotel rooms — and sometimes sleazy hotel rooms. They often left me tips, and I was often able to get high for free.

As my addiction progressed, I often found myself hiding in the dressing room, getting high. When the DJ would call my name, when it was time for me to come dance on stage, I would sometimes be too paralyzed, or "stuck," as we call it, from the cocaine high to make it to the stage to perform.

When I was first smoking cocaine, it wasn't yet called "crack." Freebasing was what they called it. But there was nothing free about it, and it had me for sure.

After I was fired from any strip clubs worth working at, I burned my bridges one by one, unable to control my addiction.

As it grew, I needed more and more cocaine more and more often. I was going home with men, then, and at last I found myself walking down streets in seedy areas, passing the girls on the corners. I was not exactly standing on those corners, yet, but I was walking on them as cars passed by.

If someone would offer me a ride, I would say yes, get in, and then get paid for my services. Starting out, I only took a ride if one was offered. I would have a real place I was walking to or from. But before I knew it, I had regulars picking me up, so it was easier to make that cash, which was going to feed my addiction. My addiction grew fast, to where I was no longer able to pay rent or for a hotel. Eventually I just walked away from everything and lived on the streets, as my disease kept demanding to be fed.

I need to stress here that most do not plan on prostitution. Most are there either to make money for survival or to feed an addiction. It was certainly that way for me.

***

Each guy wants something different and is there picking you up for different reasons, so each car is a new stage. But prostitution is not for pleasure, at least not for the female.

Naturally enough, everyone assumes that if you're a prostitute, you must love sex. However, in my 20 years on the streets, I didn't meet a single prostitute who was there because she was crazy about sex. We detach ourselves from the sex. We're like actresses on a stage, using our street names. I had a street name, and that helped me detach. I was called Ellie. Ellie was what I did; Christine was who I was.

Not everyone on the streets "plays nice." It's very territorial between streets or neighborhoods, and even on the same block. There are differences between working for yourself or for a boyfriend, someone you give your money to. The territorial nature of the street increases the risk. You not only have to worry about your safety with your tricks, but also with other prostitutes and their pimps if you cross a line.

There's a hierarchy in prostitution. It's different from street to street, and there are obvious differences between those who are homeless and surviving on the streets and those who are professional call girls. From my life on the streets for nearly two decades and in three different cities across America, I can tell you that discrimination among neighborhoods is large as well, and that plays into how you're treated. You'd better not make your money on one street or strip and then spend it on another block or with another set. If you do, you'd better not show up again in the same place.

This is why the others on the strip, the people in your set, are so important. These might not be your standard relationships, but they're essential for survival. My set, my street friends, were so important! They helped me cope. They helped me survive. Even if it was just the dope man driving by, handing me free dope and a McDonald's burger because he hadn't seen me in a couple of days, at least it was someone who cared if I was alive.

I have a group of friends that survived the streets beside me — all of us just existing back then, not living. We're still very close to this day. There's a bond that we share, one which many could never understand.

In case you're wondering about this particular aspect of being a prostitute, you won't hear me touch on fear of sexually transmitted diseases in this book. I'm sure that must be shocking to some, but the guns and knives on the streets will kill far faster than AIDS, and they kill much more frequently. Watching someone you know literally get their brains blown out totally overpowers the worry about STDs.

I see a definite hierarchy in humanity. I see that the

prostitutes who live on the streets are regarded as the lowest of the low. They are nobodies, nothings, objects, not even fully human. They're expendable. Women and men die all the time on streets across the nation, and usually their deaths don't even make the news.

But we are all members of the human race, and thus all worthy of care and caring.

For me, prostitution was pure economics. I used prostitution to support a $1,000–a–day drug habit. That's a lot of dates. By the same token, the men picking us up knew we were strung out and knew we had a price. Sometimes they would even challenge us, try to see how high they would have to go to get what they wanted if it was anything at all strange. But in the end, they had the money and thus the power. If the men hadn't had the money to pay us, we surely wouldn't have been on the streets. After all, prostitutes are killed on a regular basis. We're expendable. We're easy targets for woman–haters and violence.

Group culture dictates that you learn the rules of the streets to stay alive. I feel that I became immune to the violence because I had to. I can tell you the exact day and time when I became detached and realized that this was the life I was now leading.

I was just 15 years old and had once again been taken into protective custody, due to my frequent running away. At that time in my life, prostitution was still for survival, not due to addiction.

I was in a shelter for runaway children and teens, on a floor where all those who were in custody and who were receiving care and being examined were being held. There were about 16 young people, one only 10 years old, in this bay. During this time, I met another girl, who became my best friend.

She and I used to take turns going out and working tricks to bring back money for the soda and candy machines. We would buy those things and share them with the other kids. We had one watch that we shared, so we knew when to be back before the guards did a head count. We would always stay up and wait for one another.

One night, she was late. Way late. It was time for head count, but she hadn't returned. Later, one of the guards came in and told me to get up and put my shoes on. She took me to the emergency room, and my friend was there. She was dying and had asked for me. She had pulled a trick who had used glass from a broken Mason jar to slice her wrists and throat. She was bleeding out. The guard wasn't supposed to bring me to her but knew we were close, and she had asked to see me. I think the guard also wanted to give me a reality check of what happens on the streets.

She died. That was when I knew. That was when I really understood for the first time what could happen to me or any of the other girls and women.

After that, as you will read, I somehow made my way through almost two decades of prostitution, drug addiction, homelessness, and many times in jail. And eventually, shortly after I got clean from the crack, I would be stricken with a sudden illness that would leave me totally without sight and having to have both my eyes removed.

***

I do understand that I made many, many mistakes, and those were my choices. However, I'm clean and sober now, and I haven't had a new arrest in nearly a decade. Even then, it was not a new charge; it was a parole violation. Today, as I write this, I've been off parole for almost seven years.

A social worker once told me, "It is what it is," and that's a phrase I now use as a motto or even a mantra when faced with adversity. On the street, I quickly learned that violence is a part of it all. You can't change that fact, so you just have to roll with it. When I was a prostitute, I would often try to remind myself that this was what I was doing, not who I was. But it's hard with the guilt, shame, beatings, and rapes surrounding you on a daily basis, knowing that your life is dependent upon your individual survival skills.

Although the story of my life on the streets makes up a major part of this book, I feel that my real story began once I chose to fight to leave the streets and addiction, to learn to become a part of mainstream society. That long, hard road, those many bumps and challenges, that wild roller coaster ride, truly molded and shaped me, making me who I am today.

And so I invite you to join me, to take that journey with me.

Chapter 2

Dirty Secrets

Whoever says that drugs and alcohol won't make you do things you wouldn't normally do has never been an addict! Have any of you drinkers out there ever had this happen to you? You get drunk, go home with someone, then wake up the next morning to find a stranger in your bed. You scratch your head, trying to remember where you were the night before, so that maybe you can remember the person lying beside you.

Well, back when I was a dedicated addict, I went one step beyond that. Let me tell you the story.

At the time, I was still stripping in clubs. There were a lot of things about stripping that I loved. I could wear glittery clothes, I was on stage, and I was the center of attention. I had had low self-esteem throughout my youth, and being there on stage, with men wanting to come and watch me, made me feel pretty, wanted, and special.

By this time, though, I was frequently being sent home early for drinking too much and taking too many downers. Pills were an easy tip. I used to get Valium pills stuck into my belly button as tips when I was up on stage. Mix that with a few pitchers of beer, skipping the glass, and you have yourself a dancer waiting for disaster. I was also doing cocaine — but just a few times a week, not daily. To me, that was still fun. My drinking, however, had gotten out of hand.

My home at the time was a sleeping room that I was renting

at a little dive hotel. It sure wasn't much, but for me, it was home. I call it a sleeping room because I paid by the week, $45 per week. There was one shower and one bathroom on each floor of the old, three–story hotel. And oh yes — it housed only males! To disguise myself when I entered the building at night after getting off work, I would wear oversized, baggy clothes and large flannel shirts with hoodies and a baseball cap. I even bought myself a pair of Ninja Turtle tennis shoes to complete the male look.

The manager frequented the strip club where I was working at the time, and he knew my hours were late. I agreed not to speak to the folks who lived there, so he rented me a room close to the shower, the bathroom, and the entrance. I had to shower as soon as I got in, and I had to leave right away during the day to go to work, or else remain in my room.

I worked seven days a week. I would do the daytime stage, then work till closing unless I was sent home early. If I was sent home early, I would stop by the bar that was located between the club where I danced and the place I slept. I would stay at the bar, drinking, until it was late enough to enter my room at the old "all–male" hotel.

Sometimes during the day, I would be up and about. I often went to another little place to shoot pool. I had become pretty good at it after all the time I had spent playing it in bars where I danced. After all, I had to find something to do between my times to hit the stage.

Sometimes I would go there if I chose to leave work early, having already made a fair amount of money that night. Or I might go there if it seemed there was very little money to be made dancing on a particular night. Dancing is not a guaranteed income, that's for sure.

So if I left my place of employment of my own accord, I would go to this little spot to shoot pool and hang out. It was a nice little community bar. Given that I lived in that all–male hotel, where I had to dress in male clothing and keep my very long, blond hair under a baseball cap, when I would make it to this other location, it was a relief to be able to take the hat off and be a female, not worrying that I would see any of the tenants that lived in the hotel where I stayed.

I had befriended the owner of the little place, and I really enjoyed hanging out as a regular, rather than being a stripper the whole time, the way I had to be at my job. I was always being asked out, but my life was totally devoted to dancing. As a stripper, I got free drinks and pills, and I would often run into someone with some coke and would be able to get my high on for free. I was always seeking ways to get high, to escape who I was and what I felt, and I didn't dare miss a moment to do just that.

There was this one guy at the little neighborhood bar; everyone called him Peanuts. You know. He was the one with the long blond hair and the crystal blue eyes, over six feet tall. He was a roofer, so he had a tan, too. He had great teeth and a super smile. All the gals would swoon over him, but he never left with any of them. I think that was part of what made him so attractive. I never left with the guys, either. This was my safe place, and I didn't want to have to explain to anyone that I lived in a cheap, all–male hotel so I could save my money to get high!

Peanuts and I often joked together when we would run into one another at the bar. However, he didn't know I was a stripper, and we had never gone out or anything.

This night, the bar was full and the energy was high. Peanuts bought me a beer, handed it to me, and said, "Girl, if our team wins tonight, you have to marry me!" I laughed. All the gals would be totally jealous! We cheered one another, and I said, "What the hell? Sure!"

In fact, his team did win. He was the first shooter, and he knocked the 8 ball in on the break!

As the night progressed, it became one huge, drunken game

in the bar. Peanuts' team won again. The bar owner locked the doors, and we all got drunker for free. I agreed to uphold my commitment; Peanuts and I would get married. I'm not sure what craziness was going through my head that night, and I thought that surely you couldn't get married all in one day. I didn't even know the guy's name, other than "Peanuts."

Crazy, crazy, crazy.

Well, morning came. We popped some pills to sober ourselves up so we could drink some more. Now we were wide-awake drunks. We hopped in a couple of cars and went to a pawn shop for the rings. We walked to a one-hour blood testing place and then down a hallway to a judge's chambers. A couple of the folks we had been drinking with at the bar were our witnesses for the ceremony.

I don't think that he and I were ever sober or drug free during the first few days after our wedding. I was hustling money for us both to get high and to keep on drinking. About a week after we were married, Peanuts was in the paper and on the news. He was wanted on many charges of child molestation.

So, just days after we were married, he was arrested. I continued to work and drink, trying not to think about how large a mistake the previous week had been. Whenever I thought about it, all I could do was drink more and get higher.

One night I was asked to leave work early because I had popped a number of pills and had had way too much to drink. I was in a car wreck and fractured both my ankles and dislocated my hip. I had to get a number of stitches and staples in my head. I was given a large number of prescription pain killers, and I would take them to sleep through my inability to work. I was unable to pay my weekly bill at the sleeping room, and so had to stay at a homeless shelter to recover from the car wreck.

Once I was able to return to dancing, I did stop drinking, but I continued to take pain pills. Gradually, I would shift from pills to just cocaine. After that, there were no more downers for me, just the rush of the upper, cocaine. I was switching addictions to try to make my job doable and to remain alert. Can you imagine? There I was, actually priding myself on the fact that I was no longer drinking, while at the same time, I had built up a nice daily crack cocaine habit!

My addiction progressed, of course. Eventually, I was unable to control my usage and unable to dance on stage any longer. When the disc jockey would call my name, I would find myself paralyzed by paranoia from the intense rush of the cocaine high, unable to leave the dressing room to get up on stage. I was also losing weight.

Controlled by my need for drugs, I began walking in seedy areas and getting picked up by tricks. It wasn't long before I found myself on the corner full time, hustling money to stay high 24 hours a day — anything to keep me from feeling, anything to numb my emotions.

For many years after that, while I had kept getting high, I had no longer thought about that dirty little secret: my marriage to the guy who had won me in a pool game and had been sent to prison for child molestation. Then once I got clean, I found that many of the previous years of my life, all the years I had spent smoking crack, simply ran together in a big fog.

Years passed, and I never saw Peanuts again. However, secrets keep us sick. That's true for everyone, I think, both for us addicts and for non–addicts. I find that the cleaner I am, the more I move forward in my life, the more I find myself having to fix, repair, or get rid of things from my past. These are the prices many of us pay for choosing drugs and alcohol. For those of us who were sick with the disease of addiction for many years, it takes many years to heal our lives and the lives of those we have hurt and affected due to our sickness.

Nearly two decades had passed by the time I finally attempted to correct this one crazy mistake. Marriage is supposed to be a time of bliss and romance, but very clearly, mine had not been! I remember entering the divorce attorney's office, not really sure of what to say or how to begin, as so much time had passed and I had lived on the streets for so long.

I began telling the story of what had happened all those years before, trying to paint the picture for the lawyer. When he started asking me some questions, I stopped him and said, "This is where it gets tricky." That's because I couldn't remember the guy's real name, only his nickname, Peanuts.

So the lawyer asked, "Okay, then what's the date you got married?

I said, "Well, I've done a lot of drugs since then, and frankly, I don't remember the date."

"Okay. Do you at least know what year it was?"

"I'm afraid I have no idea. But I do know what state it was in, if that might be useful to you."

The lawyer didn't say anything for what seemed like forever. Then he said at last, "Well, looks like we have our work cut out for us, huh?"

He took my contact number and said he would be in touch.

Weeks passed, and at last I got a call. The lawyer had Peanuts' name, the date we were married, and his location. After nearly two decades, the guy was still in prison. The lawyer said the marriage date and then kind of chuckled. "Look at all the anniversaries you missed out on!"

I just said, "Yeah, right, anniversaries with a man who's still in prison!"

I have to say that cleaning up this particular mess–up was a very humbling experience. Sharing the experience now, it all seems kind of funny. But as I look back, I see that it was truly a mark of the insanity of the things we can do when we're not in our right minds, when we're in the grip of addiction.

Chapter 3

Cry Purple

I'd been up for days without food. Exhausted, I climbed into another trick's car. The "date" seemed to take hours. He simply would not stop. I was so relieved when he finally finished. I just wanted to get high and forget the whole deal.

But when I was telling him where I wanted him to drop me off, he grabbed me and demanded his money back. He locked the doors, and I was trapped in his car. He pulled my hair until I surrendered and stopped fighting him. I could often read people by their eyes, their tone of voice. I asked myself if this was a battle I should choose to fight. My gut said no. I was too tired and hungry.

He had my arm twisted behind my back and my hair tightly clenched in his other hand. He called me names, saying how all women were alike — dirty, filthy whores — and told me how lucky I was he didn't rid the world of my presence by killing me right then and there. Still, I didn't really feel the threat of death in my gut. Of rape, yes. Of some strong-arm manhandling, yes. But I was pretty sure this guy would not be one to take a life. He just wanted to get his rocks off for free and hated women.

After all my time and energy were spent, I was only going to get 20 bucks. It wasn't worth trying to fight him for that. So I gave him his money back, adjusted my clothes, and immediately realized that, on top of everything else, he wasn't going to return me to my corner. I was maybe 12 or 15 blocks away from where

I wanted to be.

It wasn't going to be the first time I had to walk back from a trick gone wrong. All I could hope for was that maybe a regular would be around to see me and pick me up, so I wouldn't have to walk all the way back.

He shoved me out of his car, leaving me on a gravel road with no shoes. They were still on the floor of his car.

I began walking, barefoot, but I didn't get very far before rain started pouring down. I knew of a small wooden shed nearby that I had slept in once before. I hoped to make it there and sleep for a bit unless a trick picked me up on the way. If that happened, of course, I knew I wouldn't get any rest.

But no one picked me up. It was rather odd, in fact. Hardly a single car passed by as I walked along, shoeless, in the rain.

I remember climbing into that shed in an alleyway down by Independence Avenue. That was Kansas City's well-known strip for finding prostitutes and my drug of choice: crack.

A board was missing from the side of the shed. I was only 5' 6" and was wearing a little girl's size 12. I was really skinny — just bones — so I was able to easily crawl in where the wood was missing. The weathered shed had a leaky roof, peeling paint, and a rusty padlock on the door. Inside were numerous spider webs, lots of dust, and some rusty old junk that was being stored there. But it offered me some shelter from the rain.

Once I was inside, I found a spot that wasn't getting soaked. I was just so tired. I'd been up for days, turning trick after trick, chasing the high. I fell asleep, and when I woke up, I couldn't tell how much time had passed. All I knew was that it was daytime. I might have slept for more than a day. I could tell the time of day approximately by the sun. At night, I could usually gauge time by the traffic flow. This time, I had fallen asleep and had awakened to the sun's bright gleam through the gaps in the wood.

I crawled out, eager to get to the avenue to turn a trick and get some crack. First, though, I had to find water. I could do without food; I knew that some crack would cure any hunger pangs. But I couldn't go without water. Often, just a cupped handful would keep me going for another day or so.

While I was walking along, keeping a lookout for a spigot, I saw some beautiful flowers in a yard behind a fence. Knowing that the owners must have a water hose around somewhere — and drawn by the flowers — I climbed over the fence. I remember just wanting to smell them at first. Then I saw the butterflies fluttering around and saw the sparkles from the morning dew, like tiny pearls on the petals. It was all so beautiful: the rich mixture of colors, so bright, with the thick, deep green grass that blanketed the ground in front of the flower bed. So I walked over and began picking some flowers of each color: a red one, a blue one, a yellow one, and a few purple ones. The purple seemed so calm, so peaceful and rich.

As I was picking them, a man came out from the house with a phone in his hands. He was yelling, and he had an accent.

"Get away!" he said. "I'm calling the police! Get away from my house!"

I had spotted the water hose, and I was thinking about how I really needed that drink of water. But I realized that the man would not let me near it.

"I'm sorry," I said, and headed for the gate, with the man still yelling at me about my trespassing in his yard and picking his flowers. I still had them in my hand, and I dropped them by the fence as I exited the yard. I turned as he yelled once again that he was calling the police.

"I'm homeless," I said.

Then it hit me that I was barefoot, that I was standing in the cool of the grass, and that his flowers were beautiful.

"I don't see much beautiful stuff," I said, and then I started walking again.

I realized then that he had stopped yelling at me. In fact, I heard him behind me, saying, "Hey, lady."

I turned, thinking for sure the police had arrived at his house already. Instead, I saw that he was holding the flowers I had dropped. He handed them to me.

I smiled and said thanks. He made eye contact with me very briefly and then looked down. When he looked at me again, it was with a stern glare.

"Now go," he said, "and stay out of my yard."

I remember walking with those flowers, smelling them along the way — the smell so sweet, so fresh, so pure — looking at the bright colors against my hands, which were riddled with open sores and blisters. My hands were so dirty, so dark, and the purple was standing out against them, so vibrant, clear, and bright. The color itself seemed to shout, so happy and good. The brilliant colors of the petals across my blackened, filthy flesh were so beautiful, and the smell was so fragrant and sweet!

That day, in the sunshine, I slid the flowers behind my ears as I walked to the corner where a trick was waiting, flashing his brake lights as a signal for me. My beautiful moment was over. It was back to the chase of the high.

Chapter 4

Hit it and Quit It

I've been arrested so many times that I have a rap sheet 19 pages long, with three to five arrests per page. I have a total of seven felony convictions and have made six trips to the penitentiary. Sometimes I was sent up on new charges, but sometimes you get out for a court date, and then there's a bench warrant for failure to appear — that kind of stuff. So you can end up arrested for the same charge a number of times. Of course, with my living in parks and empty buildings, sleeping behind dumpsters or even in parked cars in the winter if the doors were unlocked, running when the owner would enter the car, and never having a watch, much less a calendar, I would never make it to those court dates.

Often being up for days at a time, sometimes I would get arrested and have to ask what month or even year it was. It was another world, a totally out-of-touch world, the world of drugs. For me, at least, it meant that my drug was my god, my crack pipe was my husband, and my pocket was my pimp. My drugs cared not if I ate or slept. Day after day, I was in and out of the tricks' cars, often not eating for three or four days at a time, only sipping water from cupped hands from a water spigot after sneaking into someone's back yard, or getting some water in a public restroom.

This was also the way to clean up from all the tricks. Ho baths, we used to call them: Go into a public restroom with a fresh change of clothes bought at a local thrift store, wash up as best you can, trash the clothes you're wearing, then put on the thrift store clothes. Sometimes I was so dirty that I would just walk out of the thrift store in the 'hood, close to Independence Avenue and the dope spot where I got my drugs, with the just–bought used clothes and then change right there beside the building, sometimes ducking between cars in the parking lot. Then I'd walk back to the avenue to get right back on the corner to hustle those dollars for that hit of crack. The call of my addiction governed each and every action, every breath I took.

City jail: no biggie. I was often released in paper clothes, given that my own clothes were so filthy. I would be bare-legged and freezing, but the paper shirt and paper pants would be like a fresh new outfit.

At the city, where they do their fingerprinting and take the photos and such, you would often see a TV judge. I think that during all my years out there, at one time or another, I saw just about every judge the city had: learning if it was to be time served, or if I was to be released to return for a court date, or if it was off to Leeds, which is closed now. It was about 50/50. Sometimes I would only be held for a 20–hour investigation, so they could get enough information to find out if the arrest could be picked up by the state instead of my doing just city time. That would be a rest period, long enough to get a few sandwiches, lots of water, and as many hours of sleep as I could get.

I remember often falling asleep while I was standing there waiting to get fingerprinted, the guards having to keep me as alert as they could so they could take my picture, fingerprint me, and book me in. I had always been up for days from the drugs. When you no longer have the drugs in your system and you're still for some time, your body shuts down at last. Usually the sandwiches they gave you when you got to the jail would seal the deal. They would give them to you while you were waiting to be booked in or processed. By the time they're eaten, your body is searching for rest, for sleep....

Doing city time meant Leeds, so it would be a bus ride out there. One time I got arrested with crack. My partner had made a little run from the police when we were stopped, so I had time to stash the crack I had just scored. He was booked, and the officers said, "Ellie, you stay right here. We'll be back to arrest you." I had had a bench warrant for trespassing or something like that. I could have run, but gosh, I sure was tired. There was one cop holding a spotlight on me at 2:00 in the morning, and there really was nowhere to go. We had been in a brightly lit parking lot, walking across it to get to a store to buy a pipe to smoke the crack I had just scored. I stuffed the dope in my kitty, then my partner was caught, and we went to jail. We were so tired, and a couple of days in jail meant showers, food, and much-needed sleep.

Anyway, the next day, we were sent to Leeds. On the bus, there were about fifty guys and a small caged-in area where they had us gals. There were never more than about fifteen gals. I knew I didn't want to go to Leeds, the place where the city jail housed its offenders, with the dope, so I pulled it out and asked, "Anyone got a pipe? And a lighter? And who smokes crack?"

We were breaking off hits, ducking between the seats, blowing the crack smoke out the police bus windows on our way to jail. We all took turns: Hit it and quit it. I remember saying, "Let's everyone get their high on before we hit the farm!" Then I threw the rest of the dope out the window. What insanity!

Today, in my right mind, I dare not even think of getting high, much less doing some crazy stuff like this. But at the time, it was totally cool. I guess if you're going to be a dope fiend, you might as well be a cool one.

Chapter 5

You Could Live Through This, You Know

I've been cut with a box knife. I've been hog tied and raped, with gray tape across my face and eyes, believing I was going to die. I've been left naked by the river in the snow. I've been held at gunpoint until it no longer scared me. It was just, "If you're going to shoot me, if you're going to pull the trigger, please do it," asking the gunman if he thought I liked living the way I was.

I remember walking once, having been up for days. I'd lost one of my shoes somehow, somewhere. I was dirty and smelly from turning tricks and not bathing, from getting high and sweating and not bathing. I was hungry. A car slowed down beside me. The man rolled the window down and called me a whore. He drove around the block and came back, driving towards me this time. He cut the car and almost hit me.

Then he came up behind me, rolled down the window, and pulled a gun. "Get in the car!" he said. It was daylight. I didn't see any other cars close by for safety, so I took a deep breath. The guy said in a louder, harder voice, "Get in the car, bitch!" As I started to run, I said, "What you would do to me once I got in that car is far worse than you shooting me in the back." I ran, and he went on.

I've had knives put to my throat. I've been beaten, put in the trunk of a car, and left outside the city.

Once, when it was daylight, I was picked up by a guy who said he was on his lunch break. We went to McDonald's and got value meals. He drove us to the railroad tracks, where we sat on the hood of his car eating. He gave me 50 bucks, and when I took another bite of my burger, he backhanded me so hard I did a head flip off the hood of his car, hitting my head on the ground, knocking myself out briefly. When I got it together, I realized he had a box knife and had cut me on my stomach and my breast. When he was finished raping me, he left me.

I'm not sure how long I'd been out of it, but I managed to get up and make it to the laundromat, to get a dope man to give me some free dope. We stole someone's clothes out of the dryers, and he drove me to a house to shower and clean up the numerous cuts and bruises all over my body.

Once a guy in a truck picked me up, in the daylight, in the summer. I remember that for sure it was scorching hot. I'd been standing on the corner through most of the heat of the day. I'd taken my shoes off blocks before, when I was walking up and down the strip, in the hope that someone would pick me up. My hair had been uncombed for days, if not weeks. I'd also been without a bath for a long time. I remember the flies all around me. I remember no longer thinking about hunger; it was too hot for that. By now I was hoping I might even make it to jail for a shower and some sleep.

He picked me up in a fancy new truck. He was in his mid- to late thirties, and he had a nice smile. One thing I've learned from my time on the streets is that most of the time, a bad guy will not act like a bad guy right away. He'll be nice, so he'll get a chance to be that bad guy.

He put his window down. "You hot?" He had a bottle of water. "The AC is cool in the truck." So I climbed on in, and we drove. I drank the water. He asked what kind of music I liked, and if I was hungry. At the time, I was just hot and thirsty, too hot to think about eating. I poured water on some napkins, wiping my face and hands clean as we drove during that hot, sunny afternoon. He had good teeth, was clean shaven, had a fancy new pickup truck, and was mild and soft–spoken.

He gave me 20 bucks. "That's for food," he said, "no strings attached." Then he handed me a 50–dollar bill and said, "This is for our date." He said he'd find a shady place to park. He was in a hurry, so we drove to the cemetery down the street and parked under a tree.

"You haven't bathed lately, huh?" I'm sure the smell was even more overpowering to him. I had done trick after trick, hit after hit, with no shower in between. I looked in the side view mirror, thinking I would have to chop off my hair to be able to brush it. I picked a stick and then a leaf out of it and tossed them out the window. By now in my addiction, turning tricks was harder for me. The crack was calling me, demanding.

He said, "Let's just do a blow job, if you don't mind." So I proceeded. Then he grabbed my hair, moving my head under the steering wheel. While using his leg to hold my head locked under the steering wheel, he used zip ties to zip lock my hands. He shoved me to the floor of the truck, grabbing my feet and zip tying them as well. I was trying to scream, but he added more pressure to my throat with his leg.

The zip ties were getting tighter. He grabbed my hair and put strips of tape across my eyes, across my mouth. He threw a blanket or jacket or something over me as he used his hand to force me farther down on the floorboard. He said calmly, "The more you move, the tighter those zip ties will be. We have a long drive, and I'd hate for you to cut off your circulation before we arrive at our destination."

We drove for what seemed like hours. I was so tired, but I didn't dare fall asleep. I tried to concentrate on the turns we were taking. I knew when we got on a highway. I know we drove for hours.

When he stopped the truck, he said, "I know you're cramped down there." He uncovered me and pulled me up to the seat. Then he put glasses on my face, hiding the gray tape over my eyes. He said his windows were tinted and that we were in the country. He said he'd let me sit up for the remainder of the ride if I would be still and not fight. Then he said he'd take the tape off my mouth. I nodded my head, agreeing. My ankles still had the zip ties on them, more than one. Whenever I moved, I felt them grow tighter. As for my hands, he readjusted them so they were zip tied in front instead of behind my back. "Thanks," I said. I was crying. I was scared.

"You know," he said, "you could live through this." Then there was silence.

We continued to drive. The silence was deafening. I no longer felt the warmth of the sun, so I really had no idea how long we had driven. He must have filled the gas tank before he had picked me up or searched for his victim.

At last we stopped. He told me he would be putting the tape back on my mouth. I begged. He replaced the zip ties on my wrists with gray tape and cut the restraints off my ankles. We got out of the truck. I smelled mildew, a damp, musty smell as we walked. I walked across something plastic that had been laid over the walkway. We went down some stairs that I think were outdoors. Then we were in a room of some sort. The smell of dirt and mildew was very strong. There was plastic everywhere.

He shoved me in a corner. I heard the door slam, then lock. I don't know how much time passed. I had urinated on myself and had drifted off to sleep by the time he returned and kicked me. "Get up!" he said, and grabbed me by my arm. We walked deeper into this area where we were. He tied me to a table and raped me. Then he turned me over and put restraints across me, with my feet on the ground. Now there was tape across my mouth and my head to hold me down and still. He sodomized me for what seemed like forever, and then it stopped and he left.

I could hardly get my legs to hold me up, I was shaking so much from pain and fear. When he returned, I smelled fire, and figured he was going to leave me here to die. Then there was the burn, the pain. He put a hot iron or something to my butt cheeks. I smelled the burning flesh. Then it stopped and he left again.

I was unable to hold my body weight; my legs had given way. I was still taped and strapped to the table. He returned and threw what must have been large buckets of water on me. Then he moved me and locked me up again. Somehow, I found sleep. When I woke up, my clothes were dry.

At last he spoke again. "Get up!" he said. My legs were shaking. I was in terrible pain. I was hungry and scared. I felt as though I had bugs crawling on me, but I wasn't sure. He threw some pants at me and said he was going to help me get them on, which he did.

Then he re–taped my legs and carried me out. I had no idea what was coming next. He put me in the truck, covering me with a blanket. We drove. "Are you scared?" he asked. I nodded my head yes. Then he asked me if I wanted to die. By now I was sure that days had passed since the beginning of this whole ordeal. I hurt so much, and I was scared.

"It's your lucky day," he said. "I'm going to let you live. But I know how to find you." He told me he had been watching me for weeks, and he knew no one would come looking for me. Then he even told me about some of the cars I had been in and about some of the corners I had stood on, and even the last day I had changed clothes. I was full of fear.

We drove on and on. When we stopped, he said he was going to untape me and let me out, but for sure he would find me and kill me if I said anything.

He did; he untaped me. It was dark. We were in that old, empty, closed cemetery, blocks from anyone. He shoved me out of the truck. My legs were shaking from pain, and my face was raw from him ripping the tape off. I felt the air on it once again, after days with the tape across my eyes and mouth. I began wiping the oozy, caked–on crust from my eyelashes, squinting at the brightness of the lights.

Then I saw that he had no license plate on the back of the truck.

I began walking back to the avenue, my hands in the pockets of the sweat pants he had thrown at me and had helped me to get on. I realized then that he had put the money he had given me in the beginning in the pockets: a 20– and a 50–dollar bill.

I walked past an open gas station and grabbed some food and a soda. I got some ibuprofen and called my dope guy to pick me up and give me a ride the rest of the way. I knew that once again, my god, my crack, would soothe the pain. It would remove me from the fear I had felt.

Chapter 6

Just Don't Call Me "White Girl"

In the city jail, if you're given any length of time to serve, you do it in a large room like a gym. There are metal bunks placed toe to toe. At each bunk, there's a small metal opening, about the size of a shoe box, where you keep your belongings. There are about 60 women in one large room. You're there 24 hours a day, minus the time when you walk out to eat in the chow hall. In the city, the men do the cooking and serving, and the women do the laundry for all the inmates.

There's bread, always lots of bread with meals: two slices with each meal, three times a day, so that's six slices of bread a day, and always lots of noodles, too. We inmates joke about it being "blow-up food." The servings are large, too, plenty to fill up on. You can put on 10 pounds a week if you eat each meal in the city.

In the city, going outside is rare, only once a week or so. But you get one free phone call a week for five minutes. That is, you don't have to call collect. You're also allowed to mail two free letters each week. Now I'm talking about the city jail. As I'll be detailing for you, city jail, county jail, and prison are all very different from one another.

In city jail, you can have a visit a week, and it's pretty simple. It's from behind glass, and it's only for 15 minutes, but you can have this each week.

Most folks are in for traffic-related stuff or for drug-related stuff: like being caught with a crack pipe. Or you can be in for having too many trespassing charges. And prostitution.

There's one TV in the room where everyone stays the whole time. Some folks sleep all day and night. Some sleep by day and are awake when it's silent at night, sitting in the bathrooms reading books by the bathroom lights. I always hated the city bathrooms: five rows of toilets, no walls, no doors. Women are different than guys. We have periods, and I'll be frank: I do not care to see another woman changing her tampon while I'm peeing. Nor do I care to sit next to another gal taking a poop. And this comes from the girl who peed outdoors for years, or climbed into dumpsters to poop outside.

Then there are the showers. There's one shower head with five sprays that come on, and no shower curtain. It's one big circle, with five shower heads spraying out water. The women shower all exposed to each other.

There are far more blacks than whites in the city jail. Many times when I would roll through, they would say, "What's up, Ellie?" But often, I would just be called "white girl."

One night I had had enough. Out of a total of 58 women, there were six white gals there including me, and all the rest were black. Of course I've gotten high with black women, and we've co-existed on the streets, but all together in this jail setting, it often feels like us against them. That's tricky for me, as I attempt to not see color. We're all created by one God, and he loves us all. And on the streets, where survival, mere existence, is a daily matter of life or death, we're all equal.

Being called "white girl" one time too many, while I was attempting to find words in a word search book I had located, I stood up on my bunk, cupped my hands to amplify my voice, and said, "Listen up, folks. My name is Christine." I started pointing at each white girl in the room, pointing at their bunks through the rows of women. "Her name is Amy." And so forth, announcing each of our names. "Our names ain't 'white girl' or 'whitey.' Now if each of you chooses not to be addressed as 'black girl' from this moment forward, which I know won't go well, you can call me bitch, ho, or Mary Sue, for all I care, but just as each one of you has a name, we do, too."

The officer yelled as she moved forward fast. "Off that bunk! Are you trying start a riot?" The officer was black, too.

"No, ma'am," I said. "I'm just sharing my name with the rest of my fellow inmates." Then I lay back down and returned to my book.

I did the last 14 or so of my days there without being called "white girl" again.

Chapter 7

Comfort

I had just gotten a six–month sentence to the city. There was this one guard; he and I kind of had a thing. On the streets, he'd pick me up to turn a trick, so when I was in jail, he'd keep money on my books. He would bring me candy and top–of–the–line makeup and perfumes from the outside, the best of contraband.

This time when I was booked in, I was very underweight. They sent me to the doctor for a checkup to make sure there was nothing wrong with me other than malnutrition. If the city took you to the doctor, you signed a statement that you'd call when your appointment was done. You were in a navy shirt and navy pants. The clothes had a huge "MCI" on them, for Municipal Correctional Institution, but you were left uncuffed and unguarded. You had to call, and they'd return to pick you up and return you in an MCI van. It was kind of an honor system.

As I exited the doctor's office, I had every intention of walking out and calling someone to bring me a change of clothes, of returning to the avenue to get my high on until I got caught again. But to my surprise, there was my friend in uniform. He asked me if I was done. I said yes. The doctor had prescribed extra meals and some daily vitamins, and he wanted me to return in 30 days to see where my weight was. My friend said, "Let me take you back." That was because there was a guard from the city there. I had my MCI clothes on, so no one thought there was anything suspicious going on.

We got to his truck, not the MCI van.

"There's a sack of clothes behind the seat," he said calmly. "They might be a little big. Are you hungry?"

Of course I was. So we drove to Hardee's. Meanwhile, I changed clothes, ducking down on the floorboard. Once we got through the drive–through, he pulled over and threw the MCI clothes in the dumpster. Then we went to a park and ate together.

This time I'd gotten a six–month sentence. Normally I just got 10 or 21 days, just enough time to eat and catch up on my sleep, to get re–energized before I returned to the corner, where I was called the Queen of Spruce, atop Hooker Hill on Independence Ave.

My friend Blue was what we called him. He asked me where I wanted to go, telling me that he was off the next two days. He reminded me that I had six months to do at MCI. I could return there, he said, or he could drive me anywhere I wanted to go. He even said that if it was too far to drive, he'd purchase me a Greyhound ticket.

"Oklahoma City," I said. I knew the streets there, and even at that very moment, all I could think about was getting high. He saw my hands shaking, and he gave me 20 bucks. I called my dope man, told him I'd just escaped and was leaving town. I bought some dope, and Blue bought me a pipe. I smoked crack in his truck on the way to Oklahoma, crouched down on the floor of his truck.

"It's a six–hour drive," he said. "I'll drive you." So he did, and then he dropped me off with $20, a couple of changes of clothes, and some sandwiches. "Good luck," he said. "I really hope you take this chance to make some changes."

Needless to say, I was totally freaking out. I'd just escaped from jail — with the help of a guard, no less. All I knew was that it was a city jail, so they couldn't cross the state line to

Oklahoma to get me. They could only get me if I returned to Kansas City. Laws and rules are so different among all jails and levels of the system!

It's funny how a drug addict always knows another drug addict, or how to find the tracks. I had worked the tracks in Oklahoma back in my stripping days. After a car wreck, I was unable to return to dancing. I was living in homeless shelters after months of being on crutches, and when I was able to walk again, I started working Robinson. That was the hooker and dope street of Oklahoma City. After a few weeks, I was doing dope, so I knew the layout well.

Now I figured I might still know some of the folks on the streets. Sure enough, I did hit a couple of tricks, find a couple of familiar faces. Then I had to find a spot. After I made my money, I could get my high on. I made a fast friend, and we went across town, where I met a great little couple. They had a house, and they liked to get high. So I said, let me shower and sleep here, and I'll hustle the money and dope so you can get high.

It was great. In no time, I hooked up with a couple of dope men, being that I had that built-in, portable, 24-hour ATM, as I referred to myself. I was like the Energizer Bunny, turning trick after trick. I was sleeping maybe one or two days a week. But after a couple of arrests there, there was one night that sent me back to KC, even willing to do my time in isolation — or the hole, as we street people call it.

I had been up for days and had gotten a cold, so I had showered and eaten and had then gone to sleep. I wasn't sure how many days I had been out. When you go days and days without sleep, just grabbing a few hours at a time, then doing it all over again, after a few weeks of this, your body shuts down. We call that a crack coma.

These times can often be dangerous for a woman, as you're in such a deep, unaware state that you're an easy target for gang rapes. You can even be taken and killed, used to make a snuff film. But that was in KC, and I was in Oklahoma. I just didn't seem to face the same threats to survival that I had in KC, which was much faster and more violent.

So when I woke up, I called my guy. He said they'd been worried about me. I said I felt better, but asked if I could get a motivator. That's some free crack to get you up and going. I'd been asleep for days and was hungry. There was no food, so I was going to have to make it 12 blocks to the set to make my cash. He said sure.

Meanwhile, the folks whose home I was using called another dope man that I used as my back–up dope guy. He said, "Girl, you had us worried!" I just said, "Why, are you late on your house payment?" He laughed, as I'm sure my cash was paying for a house and his kids' Nikes each month.

"Do you need anything?" he asked. "Yes," I said, "and some food, too." "KFC?" he asked. "Sure." So he too was on his way.

I was realizing now that I'd been asleep for nearly four days without even getting up to go to the bathroom. Now I could see why they'd been worried. I had a fever and still felt poorly, but I knew that a bite to eat and then a hit would make me forget I was sick.

Within 45 minutes, there were four dope men at our spot and my bucket of chicken. My having just gotten a few days of sleep meant I would be working 24 hours a day for another couple of months, with just a day of rest here and there.

The windows were open, and I was wrapped in a blanket. One of the dealers gave me a 20 of crack.

"Man, you really don't look so good," he said.

"I'm cool," I said. "I just need a hit."

I remember all of a sudden getting a strange wave of something.

"Something's wrong," I told the gal we called Mom. "I know this is going to sound weird, but I smell someone."

"What?"

The breeze from the window had drifted over me, and I smelled men's cologne. It hadn't come in with one of our guests, so I knew something wasn't right. My senses and instincts were a big part of how I had survived on the streets for so long.

Then it happened. I was sitting in a rocking chair facing all our guests except the last dope guy, the one who lived down the street. He was standing beside me, having just handed me my motivator, a chunk of dope that I wouldn't have to pay back. He knew that that piece, along with the dope from the others, would get me out there on the tracks, making money to get more. The thing with crack is, once you get a hit in, you want to keep getting high to avoid the huge, deep crash when the high wears off. That's the chase. Get more before the crash.

There was the bang of the police kicking their way in — at least at that second, I thought it was the police. There I was, still sick with a high fever, just waking up after four days of sleep, not yet high, with a handful of dope and a pipe in my other hand, when I heard gunshots. *This is no police kick-in*, I realized. The dope man standing beside me had been shot in the head at point-blank range, and I had brain matter on me. The other folks in the house had leaped out the window, but I couldn't get to it from where I was positioned. The masked men in hoodies continued to shoot.

I curled up into a ball in the corner. I was watching my partner get murdered, half his head gone but his body still heading for the door, while I was still clenching my crack in one hand, the pipe in the other. I realized that one of the hooded gunmen was walking towards me. We locked eyes. He grabbed my ponytail and picked me up off the ground, our eyes still locked. I was still clutching my crack, and I was gripping my crack pipe so hard that the glass broke and cut my hand. I felt the warm blood running across my fist.

I heard sirens in the background. The gun, the very gun used to kill my partner, was now against my temple. I could feel the warmth of the gun barrel and could smell the gunpowder. Then he let go, and I fell to the floor. Silence. I looked at my friend's body, which was still trembling.

Then there was stillness. Everything seemed to be moving in slow motion. I dug out my lighter, listening to the sirens. Were they coming here? I wiped the blood from the pipe. There had to have been a dozen shots fired. I hit the chunk of crack — escaping the fear, forgetting what had occurred just seconds before. I curled up in a corner under my blanket, to cover the light of the lighter as I hit my dope. Then I put the lighter in my pocket.

The sirens seemed to be getting louder. Was it the rush of the dope? I focused for a few seconds.

No. I heard voices. It was Mom's voice and those of the others, the ones who had made it out the window. I heard them crying outside the window, which was still open. The wind was blowing the sheet that was lightly draped over it. The gleam of the street light made the white sheet glow. I waited.

Then I heard, ""Where's Cricket?" That's one of the street names that I used in Oklahoma.

Mom yelled, "She must be dead! She was alone in there with them...."

Now I knew for sure that I was the only one there with my dead friend, and I tried to yell. The first time, no sound came out. Nothing. I tried again. I could still hear the sirens. Then, at last, sobbing, I cried out, "I'm here! Please, someone get me out of here, please!"

My friends grabbed me. They were wiping me clean, changing my shirt, as we moved towards outside. I was staring at our now lifeless friend. They were pulling me. "Move faster, Cricket, before the police get here!"

We stood together outside. Helicopters, cops, and reporters were all arriving. Before they got to us, we all agreed to not let them know that I had been in the house. Our story was going to be that we all got out the window as the shootings were happening.

Each of us was placed in a separate police car, so we couldn't speak to one another until the police had a chance to talk to each of us. I was the only hooker and real dope fiend of the bunch. We were all in the backs of the police cars for hours, so I lay down and went to sleep.

The medical examiner arrived. Our friend had 11 gunshot wounds. I woke up when they got me to the police station. It was dawn. We were all separated from each other, but we all told the same story. There were news reporters everywhere, with the police blocking them, keeping them away from us. I was sweating. Sick.

The officer offered me donuts and a blanket and asked if I needed to see a doctor. "It's just a bad cold," I said. "That's all. With the fever, it'll surely break." I was just then realizing that I was in the police station, being interviewed about a murder, and that I was still holding my broken crack pipe clenched in my fist.

Nine hours later, the police let us all go. That time, we were in two cop cars when they dropped us off. They told us the gunmen could come back for any of us.

Lead stories in the paper and on TV, day after day: Worst crime in years, masked gunmen. That's all we were hearing.

I called a regular trick and asked if I could crash at his apartment for a bit till I figured out what to do. He didn't get high. I could rest and recuperate from the cold. He went to work and I hustled money all day, then returned in the evenings, got my dope, got high, then did it all again the next day. But this way, at least I could sleep each night.

The cops stopped me from time to time. "You're the gal from the shootings," they would say. Yes, it was wild for sure.

About a week passed, and I chose to return to KC. Everyone knew me there, but yikes, I was just a simple, homeless hooker. However, even if I had to do the time in isolation for escape, that was where I was off to. I hitched a ride.

Two days later, I had an officer say, "Hey, hey, it's Ellie Mae! And I bet you're going to the hole today!" Ellie Mae was my Kansas City street name.

Indeed I did go to the hole. I got 15 days for escaping, and then I did another 100 days on the six–month sentence.

And indeed, I think I almost found comfort there.

Chapter 8

Jasmine

So, by now, you've seen that life on the streets is not really all that glamorous or exciting. For me, at least, prostitution was no "Pretty Woman" story. Keeping those times in the forefront of my memory reminds me mainly of bad stuff, not any thrill of the streets.

Sure, there is a certain thrill of adrenalin that runs through you during high-speed chases, when you get away without being arrested. Or maybe you're given money to get dope for a trick who's unable to score his own dope. You run in the front door of a dope house and then out the back, stealing the guy's money and the dope as well, sneaking away to make it somewhere to get high. Or there's just the pumped feeling of wondering how to get your next few dollars to get your next high.

We addicts often say that the streets themselves can be an addiction.

Everyone knows us, so we pass around our hits. After making a big score, we think we're cool as a dope man gives us a "double up." That's $40 worth of crack for 20 bucks. Then all your street buddies are amazed and want you to get *them* that much crack for their $20.

When you're cleaned up and working and making money on that corner, everyone wants to be your buddy. They call your name as they see the car you left in return. They greet you with a smile. You feel wanted, and although you know it's for the crack they know you're about to buy with the money you just made, it still gives you a sense of belonging.

Jumping in a car, you're not sure what the pay will be. I mean, there are certain regulars. You know them and what they pay, and you know they're safe. Sometimes you turn a trick for $20, and sometimes it's for $100. You just never know. Or maybe it's a guy with a pocketful of money just trying to get high, and he wants you to help him.

If a guy I was with got high and then "stuck," unable to drive or even speak, I would often get his keys. Then I'd get the dope, his car, and his money. Then at least I'd be off my feet for a few days, watching out the rearview mirror for the police or the man whose car I had taken, leaving it abandoned a few days later, or letting another junkie have the keys and risk being stopped in it.

Now I'll share with you a story that even today makes me sad, because it's so painful. It's a prime example of just how far gone I once was, just how far my disease of addiction would take me, leading me to places and to do things I never thought I'd be capable of. But addiction is progressive. The longer you get high, the less you consider the consequences, and the easier it is to take rather than hustle to earn your money.

I remember being really tired, much more than usual, just wanting to sleep. I had done drugs for years, but now I was finding myself crawling under the tables in laundromats at night to just sleep. What was going on with me?

I had been picked up on a ticket and had gone to the city jail. I remember falling to the ground in the police station as they asked me to stand against the wall until my name was called to be booked in. I was taken to the emergency room. I was dehydrated and severely underweight.

They came in later and told me I was pregnant. Really? Gosh, how many tricks per day had I been turning? On average, three to five an hour, often 24 hours a day.

"How far along am I?" I asked.

They told me I was so underweight that it would be hard to tell, but they ordered an ultrasound to try to get a better idea. They brought me sandwiches and some Sprite, and I waited. By now, all I wanted was a hit.

Oh my gosh, I was thinking, this can't be real! God only knows who the father is. I sure didn't have a clue. It could have been any one of hundreds of men. I thought, I'm living in a park, sleeping in empty, abandoned buildings. I can't be a mother! I'm a full-blown crack addict. I didn't even know what year or month it was.

They returned. "We think about 12 to 14 weeks, but it's hard to tell." They explained to me that that was due to my own low weight.

I thought to myself, *At least three months pregnant? Are you kidding me?* The jeans I had on were a size 0, and I needed a belt to hold them up. My mind was racing. All I wanted was to call the dope man right then and there. I just needed all this to stop.

I was returned to the city jail. I believe I did 10 days, and then I was released.

A few days after my release, rumor had it that someone was looking to clean up a couple of girls that hustled the streets to work for their escort service. The people running it were a woman and her boyfriend.

It was late fall, and I was pregnant. I had to make some changes. I asked my friend to give me the number, and I stuck it in my pocket. I had been a renegade, a soldier, as we called it: just doing my own thing day after day, hustling money and getting a hit whenever I wanted it. If I were to try this kind of thing, I'd have to follow rules, I assumed. But what kind?

We on the streets call folks that run these houses "house pimps." They keep the money. They arrange for the tricks and the dope, but there are rules, and I didn't abide well by rules. I knew that sometimes the consequences for not following the rules in these places were very severe: beatings, being locked in rooms or closets, or even death.

But I was so tired! Not even a hit of crack was giving me energy anymore. The baby I was carrying was zapping every ounce of energy I had.

It was raining steadily the night I finally chose to call. I was out turning tricks in the rain, looking for dry places to get a hit on my crack pipe, trying to keep my lighter dry enough to work. When the sun came up after that long night of rain, I called the number I still had in my pocket.

We talked on the phone, and we made an agreement. It's true; we street folks do have certain loyalties to our word.

I happened to know a few folks who knew the woman, so I told her I was letting them know where I was going. I said I would give it three days, and if I couldn't do it, I would return to the streets. Then I told my friends that maybe I'd return in three days. I would either continue with this woman in her business, or I'd be back.

The first thing she did was ask me if I was hungry.

"Why?" I asked her in return. "Are you already trying to run up a bill that I'll owe you?"

She smiled kindly, making eye contact. "Nope, but if you're hungry, we'll stop and get you some food before we go to the house. It's on me. No strings attached, I promise."

"You got a piece of paper?" I asked.

"Sure, but why?"

"For the next three days," I said, "I want you to write everything that I owe you on that piece of paper. I'll sign it each time, showing we both agree. If something is free, then I want that listed on the paper, too, with your signature on it. I'm just trying to keep both of us honest."

Truth was, there was this guy I knew about. I'll use his initials, H. C. He had a few of these houses. I had heard that he would pick a girl up, buy her food and clothes, and let her get high for free. Then, like a light switch being flipped, the kindness would be gone and you would owe him. He would keep you in debt to him, so you were trapped.

I know one gal who had been beaten and pushed down a flight of stairs. He took her to the ER, got her fixed up, let her heal, kept her locked up for a while, and then put her right back to work. Another gal that was working the streets with me at the time said that she had worked for him for a while, too. When she owed him, he knocked out her teeth, took her to a dentist to get her dentures, and then she was back to work for him. He would buy her eyeglasses when she needed them, clothes, and a car, but it was a trap. Basically, you did what he expected of you, no matter what, or you would face very severe consequences.

I was determined that I not going to be set up like that, and she agreed.

Then she said, "You've been on the streets a long time, huh?"

I remember thinking, Like it really matters to you!

Then she was silent. We went to the drive–through window at a fast food place, and she wrote the cost of the food on my piece of paper. Then we went to her home.

The house was very pretty. Two other gals were there, but I could tell they were not off the streets. They were dressed really nicely, and their hair was done. There are different breeds of prostitutes for sure.

They welcomed me and invited me to sit at the dinner table. The house was set up like a regular home. It was clean, and there was art work on the walls. I didn't smell drugs.

When I had finished eating, they asked me if I was still hungry. I was. So they brought me more food, and then they showed me around the kitchen. They had a large freezer with all kinds of food in it, also cabinets filled with junk food and snacks and sodas. All I could say was, "Wow!"

"Eat what you want," they said. "Just be sure to put your

dishes in the dishwasher when you're done." They explained that we would each take turns at the end of the day making sure all the dirty dishes were in the dishwasher, and then it would be started before bedtime.

"Bedtime?" I asked. "We have bedtime?!?"

"No bedtime," they said, "but 10:00 is a good time to be in your room. We'll talk more about that tomorrow."

The woman handed me towels and a change of clothes, and then she showed me the bathroom. It was also very pretty, with every kind of shampoo, body spray, lotion, and makeup you could think of.

"We don't have any clothes small enough for you," she said, "but we can go to the store later and get some after you have a chance to clean up."

I remember soaking in a bubble bath and then taking a shower afterwards. The soaps smelled so wonderful, and the hot water felt so great! But I remember thinking, *They can't really be that nice!*

There was a knock on the bathroom door. *Here we go!* I thought.

It was the woman again. She laid a small chunk of crack on the counter, along with a brand new pipe and a lighter. And she had brought my piece of paper with her.

"I know you're used to getting high all the time," she said. "This is free, I promise. No strings attached."

I got out of the tub and took a hit. It was even good crack.

I came out, still with my crack and pipe. I had placed them in my pocket. She said, "I'll show you to your room."

I walked in. It had a TV, a dresser, a bed with a pink bedspread, a radio, and a little box.

She said, "This little box has condoms in it." There was another little box inside a drawer. "This box is for your dope and pipe," she said. "All I ask is that you don't get high when dates are here. Now you need to get settled in." She handed me a clock. "We'll leave for the store at 5:00, so be ready to go."

"Okay," I said.

I got high, and then the girls came to the room, inviting me to see their rooms. They were set up really cool. One girl said she had been there for four months. The other said she only worked there on weekends, then went back to her house. So she didn't have her own room, but there was a room she used. It, too, was very nice.

We went to the store, and the woman said, "Pick out some clothes and whatever makeup you'd like to use. And do you want to color your hair or anything special like that? If you do, we'll buy some hair color and the girls will help you do it. And if you decide to stay after the three days are up, I'll take you to get your nails done if you like. By the way, whatever we get for you today is yours to keep if you choose to return to the streets."

I was careful to pay attention to prices as I made my selections, just in case it was a trick. If I was going to end up owing, I wanted to keep track.

When we returned to the house, she told me there was a date on his way, so we would all get ready and sit in the front room. Whoever came in would choose the one he wanted, and that girl would take him to her room for the date. Then the guy would leave.

I was the one he chose. We dated. He left money and then left.

I gave the woman the money when he left. She said, "You want your cut of the money in cash or crack?" Then she said, "You can't buy your dope anywhere else, now. You have to buy it from me. If you choose to have your own money, you can buy your crack from me."

I chose half crack and half cash as my payment. That was just in case I was leaving when my three days were up.

I turned a few more dates that night.

Then she said, "We run a mid-day special here. That means

we don't turn dates between 3:00 a.m. and 10:00 a.m. Then from 10:00 a.m. until 3:00 a.m. the next day, you'll need to be ready to work at any given time."

At 3:00 a.m., ending time, she placed some dope on the dresser. "Good night," she said.

"What's that for?" I asked,

"Don't worry," she said. "It's free. You spent some money with me, and you made money all night. So now you can relax and get high. Sleep tight, and we'll start again in the morning."

In the morning, I was throwing up in the bathroom. That's when I explained that I was pregnant.

"Then you're gonna stop getting high," the woman said.

"I don't think I can."

"Well, let me know if you need anything."

I chose to stay after the three days were up. In fact, I stayed for almost two months. Then I was arrested by an undercover officer. They took me to the county jail.

When I went to court, they didn't have enough on me to keep me or convict me, because I hadn't taken the money or even negotiated the price for my services. So the charges were dropped.

The judge then told me, "You won't be released."

"What do you mean?" I asked.

He explained to me that I was being held with no charges, but the baby I was carrying was being protected from me. I would remain in custody until the birth of the baby.

"You can't do that," I said. "You can't hold me without charges."

"Lady, I just did," was his answer.

He informed the county officers that he was to be notified when I went into labor and again at the time of delivery.

Then he said, "Ms. McDonald, at the time of delivery, you'll be free to go if the baby is tested and found to be drug free. But if the baby tests positive for drugs, I promise you that the state will bring charges against you. So you'd better hope that I've taken you into custody early enough for the crack to get out of that baby's system. If not, then I assure you that I'll make an example out of you and make sure you get the maximum time I can give you."

I was in total shock. That was in late 1999. I had the baby in March of 2000. I remember getting double trays at mealtime to ensure the baby grew. I remember drinking gallons of water, too. Following my own mindless logic, I was trying to flush the drugs from the baby's system.

I would peer out the window, just obsessing on getting high. At the time, I couldn't think correctly. Reality was very far from my thinking. I would lay out my plans to get high as soon as I was released. I was even thinking about the order of the dope men I would call.

Then I went into labor. Given that I had spent every waking hour thinking about getting high again, I was excited that the baby was going to be here at last, that I was going to be able to get high again after three and a half months with no dope.

I remember them shackling my ankles to the bed in the delivery room, and the nurse asking, "Do you guys really have to do that?"

The officer said, "She's ours until that baby comes out and we get the stool sample from the baby to see if it's positive for cocaine."

The guard from the county that was with me knew me from my many times in and out of the county jail. While I was in labor she asked me, "So what are you going to do after the baby arrives?"

I said, "I'm homeless. You know I can't care for a child."

The big baby arrived at last: 9 pounds, 8 ounces. "It's a girl," they said.

The doctor said, "Hey, can you take off these shackles? She's not getting up for a while."

The guard did that, and then she moved to the other side of the room, close to the door.

She picked up the phone. She called the judge, and then handed the phone to me. The judge said, "Well, honey, the baby is a good healthy size. I'll be in touch again when the stool sample comes back."

After I was cleaned up and showered, I was shackled to the bed again. The baby was in my room. I remember holding her and smelling her.

"You got family?" the nurse asked.

"Not around here."

The baby was so warm and smelled so sweet. I remember tears when I spoke to her while I fed her.

It turned out to take some 36 hours for the poop test to be done. There was also a huge amount of paperwork to be taken care of, so I was in the hospital for about two and a half days after the baby was born.

At last the phone rang. The guard answered. "It's for you," she said. It was the judge.

"You're released," he said. "The baby is drug free. You'll be unshackled right away. Someone from the county will bring you the clothes you were wearing when you were brought in."

I hung up the phone.

The guard said, "I'll get your clothes back to you as quickly as I can."

"Really? You think they're going to fit?"

She laughed. "Well, maybe not. But we're not social workers here. We detain the arrested. Surely you can call someone." She paused. "You need anything?"

"A soda with caffeine would be wonderful," I said.

She brought me that, said "Congratulations," and left.

I started calling numbers. The only ones I had were dope men. I couldn't remember the number of the woman at the escort service, but surely I could look her up once I got out of the hospital. Anyway, the avenue was just blocks from where I was.

The dealers were all asking me, "Girl, where you been?" I explained that I had just had a baby.

The guard arrived with my clothes and the 96–cent check I had on my books. The clothes didn't fit. I located a dope man to bring me some clothes.

Meanwhile, the woman handling the birth certificate had entered the room. She said, "Surely you want to call her something other than Baby Girl McDonald."

I picked up the little girl and said, "Jasmine, because she smells so sweet." I laid her on my chest, listening to her breath, feeling her heartbeat. "Jasmine Nicole." And I signed the birth certificate.

I held the baby and cried, telling her that I had grown attached to her little kicks in my tummy and would miss her, but that I was too much of a mess to care for her. Rather than risk figuring out how to get help to keep her, then using again and messing up her little life, I would leave her in the hospital. I told the sweet, warm little girl that they would find someone much better to be her parent, and that I would never forget her. I remember the tears flowing.

The dope man arrived. He handed me some clothes, then some crack and a pipe. He had to go, he said, so he couldn't give me a ride or anything, but he was giving me some dope to celebrate the birth of the little girl.

I remember him asking, "Hey, are those tears?"

"I don't know what you're talking about," I said. Then he left. I put the clothes on and took a hit of that crack right there in the bathroom of that hospital room.

I came out, looked at the little baby, and cried some more. I kissed her forehead and wished her the best of life. Then I returned to the bathroom and took another hit of crack. Then I walked out of the hospital, not even having been released, yet.

That wasn't supposed to happen until the following day.

I was abandoning my little girl and running to escape my emotions.

I made it back to the avenue. Everyone seemed happy to see me.

Just a few hours after I had walked out of that hospital room, leaving behind my newborn baby girl, I was standing on the corner turning tricks again, not daring to come down off my high. Because if I did, I would think. And if I thought, I would cry. And for me — well, crying, feeling, emotions — none of those were an option for me.

Chapter 9

Are You Kidding Me?

Once, in the city jail, I had been up for way too long. I had a pipe and gave it to a gal who was going to be released on bond that night. I had 10 days coming; that's what the judge had ordered. But when I had gotten busted, I had had a pipe on me, and it was loaded with resin. There was caked–on crack on the whole thing. But I had no desire to hold onto it for 10 days, so I gave it to a fellow smoker, the one who was being released on bond that night.

It seems she couldn't wait, so she found a gal with a lighter. She had been jailed while I was sleeping. I'd been up for days already, so I showered, hit my bunk, and crashed. I was awakened by three guards who were cuffing me.

"Where's the dope?"

"What dope???"

The gal had gotten busted hitting that pipe in the bathrooms while sitting on a toilet. As I mentioned before, we all shared five toilets, with no walls and no doors, just five toilets in a row.

In my head, I was thinking, "What was she thinking?!"

The guards made me strip off all my clothes. Then I had to squat and cough.

"Spread the cheeks!"

"I ain't got no dope," I said. "Never did."

They cuffed me wearing no clothes and put me in a dry cell,

with no water available to me. That was so they could keep track of all my bodily functions.

"Are you kidding me?" I said. "As many times as I've been here... This ain't my thing. I hit it on the bus on the way out and threw the dope..."

They let the gal go. Her bond had been posted by that time, and when she was caught, she passed the buck to me. It had actually been my pipe. But in our state, Missouri, if it's not on your person, they can't charge you with it. And the city really didn't care for all the new paperwork. But dope... Of course that's a state charge, not a city thing, so brownie points there for sure.

The day after I went to the dry cell, a male inmate was brought down the concrete halls, yelling. He was locked in the cell by mine, a concrete cell about 6' by 6'. But the walls don't go all the way up. There are no windows. My toilet and the water release for drinking had been shut off, in hopes I would drop the dope.

After they locked him down, they threw me a gown, saying, "Put this on." By that time, I'd been in the dry cell for just over 24 hours. *But they have to give me water with my meals,* I thought.

The newly locked–up man was yelling. ranting. I smelled shit. The only thing separating us was a concrete wall about six inches thick and eight feet tall. I felt sick. I heard the guards running. They had cameras on these isolation cells. The guy was eating his poop.

"Fuck this!" I said. "Get me out of here!" I yelled. "Get me *out* of here!"

I had two more days of dry cell coming, but who knew when they would release me from isolation. It became a challenge of wills. The judge had given me 10 days for trespassing and for stepping off a curb suddenly, with the possibility of causing injury to myself or others. But they hadn't actually caught me with anything this time, so whose will would hold out? I didn't have any dope on me.

I hadn't minded the isolation up to then, and I had no real worries with no dope on me. They had to test my urine to see if I had eaten the dope and check my poop to see if I had eaten the dope in a baggie. But I was only guilty of giving my pipe to a gal who was leaving as I was arriving.

I felt the drops, then the warm stream, and then I heard the laugh. They guy was peeing up in the air in his cell, in the direction of my cell. Are you kidding me? There I was, wet with this stranger's urine. I yelled for the guards and showed them that I was wet. They smelled the stench.

"Give up the dope!" the guard said, and slammed the door.

I had no running water, no blanket, and no toilet paper. When I had to pee, I had to call a guard to come collect it, so they could make sure there was no dope. I didn't get a shower, either. Fridays are the isolation shower days, but I was being dry celled, and it was Thursday. I wasn't even sure if I would get a shower.

I smelled poop again. He was pooping again! This time, before the guards came, he was peeing into my cell again. And this time, it landed in my hair. The smell was getting stronger and stronger.

The truth is that I've always been a person who savored alone time in the hole, compared to being in a room of 50 to 60 women toe–to–toe, women who are not allowed to leave that room except for 20 minutes at a time, to eat. I assure you that the hole can be great for getting some rest and peace of mind. But not this time.

By now I was in tears and screaming, "Get me *out* of here! Just move me to a different cell or something!"

Friday came. Still no shower. Are you kidding me? Now the urine smell was even stronger. He was still taking every chance to pee over the wall into my cell. Talk about a whole new definition of golden showers!

Alas. It was Saturday, I was sure. I judged the new day by the types of meals served. I was continuing to be peed on day and night by the stranger on the other side of the wall. Finally, the guards rushed his cell, and I heard they were transferring him to the mental health hospital for a 72–hour watch.

"Hey, can I get a shower?!"

They finally opened my cell. The stench was so bad that they slammed the door again. I was yelling as loud as I could to some of my friends in regular lockdown, giving them numbers of people to call. This had gotten out of control.

I was tossed a fresh gown, but I presumed I would still have no shower till the following Friday, which would also be my release day. Then just as wildly, fast, and strangely as it had begun, it ended.

On Monday morning, a guard came. "Come on," she said. She handed me a bar of soap, allowed me to shower, walked me to dress–out, gave me my clothes, and said a guard would drive me downtown and let me out at the courthouse.

She was one of my friends, or at least as much of a friend as a guard could be.

"You know I ain't never caused trouble," I said to her. "When I'm here, it's my rest time. I'm a dope fiend. I come here to catch up on my sleep. I didn't have dope when I came here. I only gave that gal my pipe 'cause she was leaving. That's the truth." Then I said, "The judge gave me 10 days on my charges. I still have till Friday, and it's only Monday."

"Just go," she said. "it's considered time served."

As I walked away, she called my name.

I turned. "Yes?"

"I'm sorry," she said. "I do believe you, and so did others. It was out of our hands." She looked down, turned, and walked away.

I never went back to Leeds. After that, county jail and state prison would be my journey.

Chapter 10

Rats Gotta Eat, Too

When was the last time I had eaten? A week? Longer ago than that? I was unsure. Usually, I tried to force something down at least once a week, and every so often, I'd go home with a trick and then get to sleep and eat more or less normally for a couple of days. Of course it wasn't out of the goodness of the guy's heart. It was for sexual favors, or maybe he was an addict, too, and needed one of us girls to score for him. Once I'd had enough sleep, a shower, and a couple of meals, it was back to the track. Nothing is free, not even a safe place to sleep.

I knew that if I could get a hit, it would be enough to deflect the hunger pangs. Addiction is so powerful, so controlling, that even if one needs to eat or sleep or take a drink of water, the addiction demands to be fed first and foremost. I think that's what's so hard for family members and friends and loved ones to understand: that crack addicts are not in their right minds. They are not in control of even their most basic human needs, such as the need for food and shelter.

This night I was so very tired, and couldn't remember the last time I'd changed clothes. I'd just been turning trick after trick, walking to get my dope, walking to get high, walking to the track to turn another trick. If I had it, I had to smoke it. I was so tired, falling asleep as I walked. Or at least it would seem that way. Often, when I was walking, I would zone out, kind of like sleep walking. Then there would be a jarring shudder, reminding me that I was in mid–step. If I were to stop, I would collapse, even when crossing the street. I know it has happened.

It was winter. I remember the cold and having no coat. I remember the little pecks of sleet that were pinging on my exposed flesh and the white of my breath as I walked. *Am I invisible?* I would wonder as I watched the cars pass.

At last one of my friends from the streets pulled up in a car. "Wow!" I said. "Whatcha doing driving a car? Is it hot?"

He told me that it was his girl's car. He'd been away from home for three days at that point, was broke, and was dreading returning home to face the music.

"Get in," he said. "I ain't got no heat, but I got a little gas. Need a ride?"

He was a crack smoker like me, but one of those with a job, so he didn't come out often. I had met him in treatment many years before.

Just like me, he wanted to get high. I said I didn't have any cash and hadn't had much luck on the end of the avenue I was working. So I suggested he give me a ride down the street a few blocks, so I could see if there was more traffic there. I jumped out on the corner and he parked down the street. I got picked up, turned a trick, and was returned to the corner. My friend pulled up and we rode to the dope house. It was a break from the wind, and it got me off my feet. I was falling asleep as we drove to the crack house, nodding off and then waking up suddenly, knowing I would get a couple more hours of wake time with that hit. It would numb me enough that I wouldn't notice the cold any longer.

My friend allowed me to sleep in the back seat of the car for 30 minutes or so, and then he woke me. I ran in and bought the crack, and then we got high. Then it was back to the corner to do it all over again.

As the sleet continued, the car traffic slowed. I was so cold, so hungry. I had nowhere to lay my head. All I could do was stay out on the corner, chasing the high till my body would no longer allow me to. No one picked me up. By this time, it had been about a week since I had last eaten, and now the hunger was outweighing even the desire for crack. My friend was out of gas, now, so until I made some cash, he was parked there in his car.

"I have to eat," I told him. "Maybe I'll get picked up by a trick as I walk up the street to the 7–11, and then I can buy some food to give me some pep to work longer."

I chose to ask for some spare change as I walked across the parking lot, totally focused on food. No luck. I went into the 7–11. I was known around there, and they had a police officer posted inside the door due to the shoplifting by folks like me, the homeless and addicted. I made my way to the cold foods section and grabbed some packages of shaved lunch meat. I knew that protein would be the best, being that I hadn't eaten in a week. My body was eating up its own muscle tissue for energy, so I knew this would be just what I needed to head back up the street and get back on that corner.

I moved fast to the door. The policeman looked at me. I moved faster, and he stepped forward. My mind was racing. *Did he see me? Is he moving toward me?*

I wasn't taking any chances, and walked away from the store as fast as I could. Then I slowed down and looked back. He wasn't coming after me. He was just standing at the door of the store. Maybe he knew I was up to something, but he didn't know what. He hadn't figured out that I had shoplifted lunch meat.

I reached into my waistband, pulling out a package of the meat, my mouth salivating at the thought of food, my mind totally focused. I was starving. I tore the package open and ravaged the food, shoving as much in my mouth as I could. I bit my finger, not moving it away fast enough as my teeth chomped down. I saw blood on my hand. I'd bitten my finger so hard that I'd drawn blood. I wiped the blood on my pants, trying hard to slow down, but desperate to eat, to chew.

My eyelids felt so heavy, as though there were little weights on the lids, bearing down. I would find a place to lay my head — that is, if a trick didn't pick me up before I made it to an empty building to find rest.

I found myself walking to a so-called honeycomb, a place where many of us went to sleep. It was a condemned building with no windows left in the frames, no doors, and some floors missing. I had made up my mind that if a trick or crack smoker didn't pass me by the time I got to the building, I would find a corner and crash, even while knowing how dangerous this could be to a female. We women would often work until we simply had no choice. When we were tired enough, then the fear was gone, and sleep was all that called.

I found my way into the building, climbed down a floor to the basement level, and found a corner where some bricks were missing. That was okay. That way, some air would move the stench of the place where so many others had relieved themselves and God only knows what else. Another name we had for these kinds of sleeping places was "abandominiums." They were common enough that all of us knew about them, but we used them only when we simply could not stay awake any longer.

I curled up, and I think I was asleep before my head hit the bricks beneath me. I'm unsure how long I slept. It might have been that same night when I woke up again, or it might have been two nights later.

The fact is, those years just ran together. Often, I didn't even know the date until I would get arrested again and then ask what the date was, what year it was. I remember police officers over the years sometimes driving by and yelling, "Hey, Ellie, do you know it's Thanksgiving?" or "Hey, it's Christmas!" Otherwise, I would have had no clue. At least I could gauge the time of day by the traffic, by the tricks' cars, by the "set." Funny, huh?

Anyway, that night in the abandominium, I remember the pain as I woke up, screaming, in fighting mode. I thought I was about to be raped, attacked, or robbed. I knew there could be one or many of them. If we female addicts fell asleep in the street, on a sidewalk, in the park, or in an abandoned building like this one, we often became victims of rape while we were in our crack comas, totally unaware and unable to wake up, sometimes for two or three days at a time. There were the junkies that would have their way with us when we were in that state, and some girls never woke up at all.

But nothing like that was happening this time. As a gleam of light came in through the missing bricks, I saw that my attackers were rats. One of them had bitten my face. I had fallen asleep in mid–chew of the lunch meat. I'm sure the winter months were hard on the rats, too.

Screaming, I squeezed myself through the hole left by the missing bricks.

Back on the block, the first thing I did was sneak into a back yard and find a water spigot. I splashed water on my face, rinsing off the warm blood that was still running down my cheek, rinsing my dirty, blackened hands, and then drinking the cool water.

All the horror seemed to stop for just a moment as my hungry, thirsty, used–up body savored the taste of the water. I often wonder if those people had a clue as to how often they may have saved me, and who knows how many others, just by having that spigot there.

The rats had to find their water somewhere else.

Chapter 11

Let Me Tell You Their Names

Rhonda. She and I would share a few years of adventures and tragedy on the streets, watching each other's backs and taking care of one another. We shared many of the same tricks, and we were inseparable. We used to joke to the guys that she had a big butt while I had big boobs, and she was brunette while I was blonde, so they could get the best of both worlds.

We felt safer being together. Often, the girls would pay a guy to watch for them. But in reality, once the girl climbed into a car, all the guy could do was remain on a street corner. So what was he really going to do once she was in the car? Then afterwards, she would have to give up half her dope to the guy as payment. I had a dope habit, so I figured, why not work with a girl, who can make money right along with you? You both got paid, you both had your own dope, and most guys that were up to no good wouldn't pick up two girls in the first place. But it did happen. We were picked up once or twice by creeps. But Rhonda and I were always able to defend each other if one of us was in a risky situation.

Rhonda drank. She loved her Mad Dog, that's for sure. We used to have the clerk at the local gas station/liquor store hold a bottle for her, so she could always grab one at any time. She needed it when she came down from a high, or when she got up in the morning.

I remember one night when we were at a guy's apartment

downtown. We used to go there to clean up, sleep, and eat. We had gone out on the track and had made some cash. We'd gotten our crack from the dope man and then had gone to this guy's house. I believe his name was Don. He worked day labor, and he always allowed us to come in from the rain or if we wanted to sleep. He kept food just for us: French fries, eggs, and hot dogs or pork steaks. It was great.

This night, we had eaten and had made a nice bit of money. We were able to get new pipes, and even got some of Rhonda's Mad Dog to come down on. We were getting high. It was night, and we were on the third floor, when we heard noise. We were both high, so any sound would make us a bit paranoid. As we heard the commotion from outside, Rhonda looked out the window.

A guy in the building across from us was outside his window. He had to be on the fourth or fifth floor. People were yelling and starting to stop along the sidewalk. After a few minutes, things seemed to have settled down, so we returned to getting high. We were both hitting our pipes when we heard a slamming thud, a sound I've never heard repeated to this day. It was almost as if the building was jarred by the thud. We exhaled the smoke from our pipes, hearing the sirens growing louder. Of course we thought they were coming to get us for doing dope.

Rhonda turned out the light and we looked outside. The man was lying face down on the sidewalk. There was blood. There was silence. He was dead. It took a bit to shake that off, but soon enough, we were back to our dope, which was waiting patiently for us.

There are many stories I could share about Rhonda and me — like the one about the sugar daddy who wanted to get me off the streets. I called him Captain Save–a–Ho. He rented me an apartment in Westport and bought me brand–new furniture, everything from a five–disc CD player to a 27–inch TV. He bought me a bedroom suite and a living room suite and paid for the rent for six months. Then I told him I would move in only if he let Rhonda move in, too. I'll never forget the day I moved into the apartment and told him I would take the keys only if I could go and find Rhonda. I went to each and every crack house until I found her. I bought $100 worth of dope and told her to come on. She did, and then the dope man moved in, too.

The guy that rented the apartment only wanted me for three hours a week. He gave me $1,500 on the first of every month and $300 every Friday. He even paid for my wisdom teeth to be pulled. In fact, Rhonda and I got an eight–ball of crack and smoked it in the back of a pickup truck on the way to the oral surgeon. After the teeth were pulled, we smoked crack all the way back to our little hidden–away apartment.

Captain Save-a-Ho would take me shopping for clothes, and I would have him take my friend shopping, too. This lasted about three months, having a safe place and someone to buy my dope. But then he figured out I was smoking crack. I had hidden this from him for a while. However, trying to control my usage to allow him to think I was not a drug addict failed in the end. So that was that.

Rhonda and I did jail time together. We did street time together, and street time is all about life or death.

Later on, Rhonda would become addicted to the needle, an addiction I didn't share. So we parted ways. We reconnected after getting clean. However, later still, she became addicted to heroin. Then she got clean for about six months, but she relapsed, and the first time she got high again on heroin after being clean, she overdosed and died.

I've had friends murdered — like Marie, a friend who worked the streets with us. I'll never forget watching the news about that. All they had to identify her by was a tattoo on her body, on a small piece of flesh. She'd been beaten, burned with cigarettes, raped, and shot. Given that she'd been shot in the face, they said that the beating and the burns were inflicted prior to her death. They showed her tattoo on the news. That's all they had to use as an identifying mark as they tried to find out who she was. Her fingerprints were burned off. She had been to prison a number of times, so that would have been a great way to ID her, but her killer or killers had made it as hard as they could. Her face was gone. I remember taking a hit and seeing the photos of the tattoo on the news, knowing that was my friend, my friend Marie.

I had other friends who had limbs severed, their body parts dumped in the Missouri river. The head of one fellow hooker was cut off and thrown in the river. Her limbs were severed and placed in a suitcase, which was then left at a popular spot for hookers to park and turn tricks. Another girl's eyes were cut out and her torso was severed.

As awful as their deaths were, what was even worse to me was the fact that these girls were nobodies, "just hookers" living in addiction, homeless girls whose stories rarely made the front page of the paper, much less the evening news.

We folks on the streets believed these girls were being used to make snuff films, movies about real-life torture and murder that would then be sold on the black market. We believed the girls were being taken away in a truck or van and murdered there. That's why so many of the murders were unsolved. The girls' limbs were severed while they were still alive, bleeding out to their deaths after being beaten. And if we were correct in our theories about the snuff films, then they were also raped and tortured. All this was for some sick folks to watch as the girls' lives were taken.

Who looks for missing prostitutes, anyway? They're such easy targets for woman-haters or sadists. They're lost, lost in their addiction, missing for months or years without anyone seeking them. And to the community? We're just eyesores, and our lives are expendable. We're nobodies.

But we know each other's names.

Chapter 12

C C and Our Bunny

My friend C C was my bunkie in prison. We used to walk together and took a workout class together. She was also someone I had worked with on the streets of Kansas City. We used to get high together and would often run into one another at dope houses.

We buddied up in prison when I was there. We had transferred to Chilly, as we called it. We wanted to be able to walk on the grass and open our windows instead of always being on lockdown. So we did. The prison was in an old school. We could get two-man cells, and they let you open the windows there.

One day when the ladies were doing yard crew, they found a nest of baby rabbits, just tiny little things. The guards said, "Just mow over them," but that was not going to happen. You have to remember that many of the folks at Chilly were lifers, having been given a life sentence: some with the possibility of parole, but many without. They were going to die there. So a tiny, cute, fuzzy baby rabbit was going to find a home on one of the housing units for sure.

C C and I chose to adopt one. We would have others, girls who worked in the chow hall, steal food for us. We'd pick grass. We had cleaned out a metal footlocker and lined it with an old towel and grass. At night when we were on lockdown, we would take out our bunny (which we had named simply Bunny) and hold it. During the day, we would go out to what we called Blubber Beach. It was where we girls could touch the grass and lie and bake in the sun — still in our prison-gray uniforms, but nevertheless enjoying the grass and the warmth of the sun. When we were there, we'd take Bunny out. We had stashed him between our breasts to get him out of the housing units. We would lie in the grass and watch Bunny enjoy it with us.

Soon, however, Bunny got bigger and needed to get out of the little locker we had made his home. At first, we had put a rolled-up towel across the floor at the door of the cell to insure that Bunny didn't make it underneath. But as Bunny got bigger, it was harder to keep him a secret.

C C and I would take turns. We worked different shifts in the prison, so it was easy for us to keep our soft, furry friend to ourselves. But Bunny grew, as all babies do, so we could no longer hide him in our bras to go outdoors. As time went on, we were leaving Bunny out more and more often to explore our prison cell. So the word got out that we had a pet baby rabbit in the state penitentiary, one we had kept and had taken care of for a couple of months.

Of course someone had to steal our joy. One of the girls told a white shirt, and our housing unit was put on lockdown. The captain of the prison camp came to our cell after the unit was locked down.

Most folks on camp called me Ellie instead of Christine, as many knew me from the streets. With my high country Oklahoma twang and long blond hair, Ellie seemed like a fitting nickname. A nickname was a little less personal on the streets and in prison, so I was good with that.

Anyway, the white shirt had us searched.

"Where's the critter, Ellie?"

There were a couple of officers there, so we knew we were totally caught. As they pulled our lockers out, Captain said, "I have no idea how you guys kept this thing hidden, but it's going."

C C cried. I had tears in my eyes, but tried to maintain an appearance of indifference so they wouldn't feel as though they had taken our joy along with the rabbit.

Bunny had become quite tame. How on earth was he to survive outdoors? It was fixing to rain. Captain was calling for someone to come and get the rabbit, and we were getting a prison violation. C C was flooded in tears after I said that Bunny couldn't make it in the wild.

Captain said, "That's not my problem. You should have thought about that before."

Then I told her that the rabbit would have died by the mower.

"That's life," said Captain. "That's how things work."

C C asked if she could please at least walk our Bunny to the fence with a guard and let him go, so that he might have a chance to survive without being killed by our prison grass mowers. No one spoke. Captain got on the radio and said, "Disregard." It was still open yard time for the rest of the prison; only our housing unit was on lockdown.

Captain said, "Get your bunny, C C."

C C and I both started to walk out, but the guard said, "Just one of you walk that bunny to the fence." Then she said, "And don't make a scene." C C, being generally more calm and laid back than I, was surely the better choice. She let Bunny go, and we never saw him again.

***

A couple of years later, I got a call. It was after I had been off the streets and had my son. He was a few months old at the time. It was C C. I still don't know how she found me. She was in a hospice and was dying of AIDS. She told me that she had known for 17 years that she had it. After she learned she was HIV positive, her aim was to infect every male she could. So she became a street corner prostitute and chose to spend her life getting high, seeing as how she had the stamp of death on her already.

I visited her daily. The brain lesions caused her to drift in and out of knowing I was present. Her family had disowned her. She called me one last time when she had a moment of clarity. It was dinnertime at our little home. She said "Christine." It was the first time in the 15 years or so I had known her that she had ever called me by my real name.

"I'm going to meet my Maker," she said. I was at a loss for words. What do you say to someone who just matter-of-factly states that they're going to meet their Maker, someone who knows they're going to die? I struggled to remain calm for my friend. I'd been visiting her for months at the hospice, sneaking her cigarettes: only one each day I visited, also candy bars and soda. I thought, *Gosh, if my friend is going to die and you guys can't do anything to save her, what's the big deal about a cigarette?* I'd sneak her in stuffed animals and also bring treats for the girl she shared a room with. She was dying, too, but she didn't have visitors, so we'd often share my daily visits with her.

By the time C C passed, everyone that was HIV positive, all those dying people, knew my name. They would tell me, "Hi!" I'd smile and say, "Hello!"

Before C C died, I asked her, "Have you made peace?"

"I have no regrets," she said to me, "no guilt for anyone I infected."

I went to see her the following morning. She was unaware of my presence. I held her hand and spoke to her, telling her stories of our past experiences in life. Then I went home, holding onto C C's smuggled-in cigarette, just in case tomorrow's visit would be better.

About an hour after I left, I got a call. It was the hospice. C C had died. The nurse said it was almost as though she had waited for that daily visit from me before she had allowed herself to drift away. Then the nurse said, "I wish everyone here had an Ellie in their lives."

I took the cigarette from my jacket pocket and put it in the trash.

After getting to know so many of the folks at the hospice, I tried to become a volunteer there. But I was a convicted felon, a criminal, and the law wouldn't allow me to come in to do such a thing.

Often, when I hear that one of our friends has died of AIDS, I wonder how on earth I didn't get infected. The tricks often picked up different girls. I'm thankful that I wasn't infected. I'm grateful for the chance of life. I guess that a power greater than I am had a different design and knew the bigger picture.

Chapter 13

Introduction to Matt

I met Matt (short for Matthew) at a halfway house after my release from prison in June of 2004. We lived at KCCC, Kansas City Community Center, the one on Campbell St. It was the first time I had ever shown up, after a release from prison, to the place the Department of Corrections had sent me. There were always stipulations on our prison release papers. I had been homeless so long that the halfway house was my only choice. I had just done a six-month bit for a parole violation I had received in 2003 after having been released to the same place, KCCC. However, I had never shown up that previous time. I had heard the stories from other inmates about the program and all the classes, and at the time, I was not yet tired enough to consider doing whatever it took to remain free or begin to live without drugs.

My release in June of 2004 was different for me. By that time, my inner self had changed. I was tired of wandering aimlessly in the streets, of not having a place to bathe. I was tired, so tired, and at last I had found that point I had heard about in treatment and in AA and NA meetings, the point at which I hurt so damned much that I was at last willing to suit up and show up, to do whatever the halfway house required. I wanted to try to find myself and a life without drugs, and I was willing to do whatever they said.

I was so surprised when I got to KCCC, in the downtown

area of Kansas City, Missouri, just blocks from Jurassic Park, which was a hot spot for hookers, addicts, and dealers and my old stomping grounds. I was nervous about being so close. However, I was not going to let anyone know I was out. I was going to at least try to make it work. I was so tired of the streets and so tired of prison. I wanted to belong.

Just two days after my arrival, I learned I would be allowed to find a job. And once I found a job, I would attend twice-weekly substance abuse classes. It wasn't as bad as I had thought it would be.

Finding a job would be an interesting feat. I had never worked, so I had no skills, just street knowledge, and no one was going to pay for that. I didn't have a high school diploma, either, and I knew this might present a problem. However, I felt that explaining why a 35–year–old woman had no work experience might be even more of a challenge.

Thirty-four applications and 11 job interviews later, I was at last given a job at McDonald's. I remember the excitement. At last someone wanted me! I remember the man who hired me. He said, "Christine, if that smile is real, you've got yourself a job." He left shortly after that and his daughter took over the restaurant. However, I remained an employee.

But back to Matt. He lived at KCCC on the men's floor. He had a tongue ring, a cute goatee, a nice tan, and a couple of tattoos. He was six feet tall, and he worked outdoors framing houses. Matt went to work every day and went to classes every night. He didn't get into the drama of the halfway house. He seemed to have direction, I assume in order to get out. So that's how we became friends.

He became my first male friend, someone not seeing me as a hooker, a dope horror, or the person to get the dope. To him, I was simply Christine, and I really liked that.

Doing all this new stuff, being drug free, doing what my parole officer wanted, following the rules, working at making new friends — all of it was awkward and new to me.

Matt eventually moved out to his own small apartment, the same apartment we would find ourselves living in one year later.

After he left, I still lived in the halfway house and worked. I used to stop and see Matt after work every day and then walk back to the Center. It was about a 10-block daily walk for me, but I enjoyed having somewhere to go and being someone who didn't do drugs. It was fun, and there was no pressure.

At last I reached the point where I could move into my own place, a small room I rented for $300 a month in the northeast Kansas City area. It was a house where they rented out each one of the three bedrooms, perfect for me. It was next door to a laundromat and across the street from the bus stop. Shoot, it even had cable.

However, I would soon learn that being alone with myself was much harder than I had thought it would be. I truly was not ready for living on my own. I was still working at McDonald's. I wasn't going to 12-step meetings, but I was not using. I would quickly learn that being alone with myself was not a good place for me. I went to work, returned to my room, and slept. For my food, I would grab a burger at McDonald's: always a double cheeseburger, but without bread. They serve it up nicely with a large leaf of lettuce and cheese slices. Anyway, I soon realized that between the streets and prison, I didn't have a clue as to how to take care of myself. All I knew how to do was sleep and shower. Other than that, I was pretty lost. I still had a bit of fog in my head from all the years of dope, plus a lot of guilt and shame regarding many people and things I had done and lived through.

One day I walked to a grocery store, walked down an aisle or two, and left, feeling that the store was a foreign place. All those choices... Then I heard the people, saw the faces. This was a store I used to walk around the outside of at night in order to get picked up by a trick, sometimes turning as many as 20 tricks a night. I felt sick. Sweat beads were pouring; my breathing was thick. Did they all remember my face? I felt almost paralyzed for a moment, and then I ran back to the house where I was renting a room.

Guilt, shame, regret, and loss were some of the emotions I could identify. I fell asleep crying that night and didn't wake up until the next night. I think those were my first real feelings. It was my first moment of real clarity, my first truly clear vision of my past, and I was consumed.

Every day, I found myself struggling with just figuring out simple stuff. My only friend during this period, the only person I felt safe with, was Matt. Looking back, maybe I could say that I was becoming dependent upon him. I don't know. But he kept me getting up, with something to look forward to each day: my bus ride to his place to leave a card, to draw a picture, or to leave sticky notes on his windows.

As my feelings for Matt grew, I would spend all the free time I could drawing sidewalk chalk pictures up to the steps of his apartment or putting sticky notes of cute pictures on the outsides of the windows of his apartment, so that when he would get off the bus and walk to his door, he would see that I had come by and had taken a few moments to make him feel special, even if I had just turned around and had ridden the bus back to my place without seeing him. I would stop by the drugstore daily and get a card, then mail it to him. They were simple cards with simple messages, just "Thinking of you," or "Have a great day," or "Smile!"

We entered into a sexual relationship, and I soon found that I was pregnant.

In the beginning, I was so excited to tell Matt I was pregnant. I was still scared, still overwhelmed with learning how to live life without drugs, with figuring out how to get over all the guilt and shame I had buried for so many years. With great eagerness, I walked to Matt's apartment to tell him the news. But for the first time in the months we had been seeing each other, he didn't let me in. He came outside to the steps. I was puzzled. I had become used to always being greeted and welcomed in. I had become a creature of habit: get up, go to work, get off the bus to leave a note or to clean Matt's place or visit, go home, sleep, and then do it all over again. The fact that he was not letting me in was out of the norm for us.

I was still emotionally young. Was that really any wonder? I had done drugs for nearly two decades, and during that time, my emotional and mental states had remained at a standstill. So my coping skills — well, let's just say they left a lot to be desired.

I freaked. "Why won't you let me in? What's the deal?" I mean, here I was going to share this wonderful news with him. It had taken me a couple of weeks just to get up the nerve to tell him. At least I was there, to tell him I was pregnant with his child, and he wouldn't let me in the door.

I remember making a scene in front of his apartment. Making scenes was my thing from being on the streets. Being loud and attention-drawing was one skill I had indeed learned. I walked away, turned, and yelled, "Oh, by the way, I'm pregnant!" Then I turned and kept walking. I was filled with rage, confused, unable to sort out what had just happened, his odd behavior. I mean, come on, now! I was happy about this. He was supposed to react the way I had planned for him to. Why hadn't he?

I had an appointment the following day for the full examination and to start prenatal care. That was when I would learn that the child I was carrying was not okay. I was not okay, either, and we would begin a roller coaster of emotions and heartache.

Matt and I talked later, and he explained what had happened that day. There had been others in his apartment, and they were getting high. Knowing I was struggling to stay clean and not return to using, he hadn't wanted to expose me to all that. He had simply felt that not letting me in was the best solution — rather than have me come in and have some kind of dramatic reaction, or expose me to the drugs. Maybe I wouldn't have had the willpower and coping skills to say no to them.

Chapter 14

On the Bridge

I spoke to Matt, and we worked out my anger about him not letting me in. We talked about my pregnancy. I would have to seek prenatal care. He told me that he had no kids of his own, so this would be his first child. He said he would stick with me through this, and he seemed excited — that is, as excited as his personality would allow. Matt was a man of few words. But I was always able to read his expressions in his eyes — to go with his words, and then be reassured by his thoughtful expressions. For me, the expressions spoke far more than his few words.

As for me, I was clean for the first time in many years. I was no longer turning tricks, and I was learning to live life on its own terms. It was not always easy, but as each day passed, it seemed that increasingly, using was not the first thought that came to mind. I still really struggled with my emotions and trying to keep a grip on them. But for the most part, I was learning to adjust. I was taking it one day at a time, glad when each day passed without my having gotten high, glad to be working my first job. Plus, I was in a relationship with a man who seemed to accept me as I was.

I spent the whole day at the doctor's office. They did blood work and a prenatal exam, then an ultrasound. They gave me some baby books and pregnancy information. I was eager to share these things with Matt and returned to the apartment.

A couple of days went by, and the doctor's office called.

They wanted me to return for another ultrasound.

I learned then that I was carrying a baby that was very ill. I had massive fibroid tumors that were a danger to the baby. Somehow they caused the flow of the blood of the placenta to be disrupted, which could cause brain damage. We wouldn't know the extent of all this until her birth. In addition, the baby had something they could detect in the ultrasound, Pierre Robin sequence. The lower cranial facial part of the skull had not developed. There are other things, too, that can occur along with this condition.

The clinic thought it best for me to terminate the baby.

What? I thought. I was struggling just to cope with day–to–day life. How could I be faced with such a situation?

Torn, feeling so alone, so wanting this baby, I was pained. Could I knowingly bring into the world a baby that might not make it? And if I did, would he or she be mentally challenged and physically deformed — to the point that it would be wrong to bring the child into the world? But could I play God, deciding to take a life? I was so new to being clean. I reflected on the little baby I had left in that hospital room years before. The thought of her still haunted me.

My heart hurt.

I was still irrational in my reactions to having to make choices of any kind. I was unable to focus, unable to clear my head enough to think rationally about my options. I just took off walking, crying, confused. I'm still not sure why I didn't call Matt, but my thinking was dominated by my emotions.

That afternoon, I relapsed. I had been clean. I was working at McDonald's and had my own place. Yet that day, I felt that only crack could comfort me. I felt that returning to what was comfortable and familiar would help me cope. At the very least, it would stop the flood of thoughts, worries, and the words of the doctor that were weighing so heavily upon me, his words about terminating the pregnancy. Somehow, somewhere in my heart, I believed that life begins at conception. In my mind, ending the pregnancy would be murder. Now, I had done many, many wrong things along my journey up to that point, but making the choice to knowingly end a life — well, in no way could I bear such a choice.

At the same time, I had awful visions in my mind of what the outcome might be for this child. What kind of life would she have? What if the worst of the scenarios that had been presented to me occurred? And would the baby always need care? She could need a tracheotomy and a feeding tube. And if the flow of the placenta was truly interrupted by the massive tumors, she would probably have severe brain damage on top of that. Also, the doctor had told me that when a child has Pierre Robin sequence, it's almost always in combination with Stickler syndrome, or Treacher Collins syndrome. Newly off the streets and clean, I felt that all this was simply too much of a burden for me. After all, I still stressed about choosing what to eat for lunch, or what pair of black pants to wear to work that day!

I got off the bus on Independence Avenue and spotted an old friend from the street.

"Ellie!" she yelled.

A wave of comfort instantly washed over me. I had been clean for 13 months, and in mere minutes, I threw that clean time away. As the night went on, I saw many more of my street buddies. They all asked me what it was like to have a job, what it was like to have been clean. They all gave me dope. Within a day or so, my new lifestyle had worn off, and I was back on the corner hustling tricks for money to get high. I had a number of old regular tricks stop and even give me more money than they used to. They all seemed so happy that I had been off the streets. So how could this odd kind of reunion comfort me?

With each hit, I would escape once more the thought of what my reality was at the time. I was running away from everything: my job, my apartment, my emotions, and Matt. I didn't contact him even once during a period of at least two weeks.

Eventually, I got stopped by the police. They ran my name and found that I was on parole. So I was taken to an honor center to await a hearing for a parole violation.

An honor center has much more structure than a halfway house. The State said that because I had had a job and had been off the streets for the first time in years, I shouldn't go back to prison, but instead needed to be monitored, that what I needed was more structure. I could only cry. All I could think about was what the doctor had said about a medical termination of the pregnancy. Then came the guilt that I had gotten high again, the disappointment in myself. How could I dare to face Matt? I had come so far, and now this! All these thoughts kept running through my head, never stopping.

I waited in the hole, isolated, for a response from the parole board. I no longer had the crack to cover my thoughts and numb my emotions. I did five days in the hole before the report from the parole board came back. I was to stay at the honor center for 30 days, getting out only to go to work each day. Then, if I didn't get into any more trouble, I would be released again to the streets.

I contacted my place of work, and they let me return. However, I had reawakened the lion of my addiction. I had brought that mental obsession to the surface of my thoughts again. For months, getting high had slowly moved down on my list of what to do when anything good or bad occurred in my day–to–day life. Now I was feeling guilty for getting high, feeling guilty for letting Matt down, and feeling just as bad about letting myself down.

So, on my first day back at work, on the way home, without even thinking, I got off the bus on the corner of Independence Avenue and Spruce Street and started getting high again. This time, though, I found that taking a hit didn't take away my extreme guilt and shame. For the first time in my life, the drug had betrayed me.

Crying, raging with emotions, I remember walking to the bridge that night. It began to rain, slowly. I felt the raindrops as I listened to the traffic below.

Then the rain grew heavier, pounding. I felt so lost, and I had no one to turn to.

I couldn't stand the pain. I stood there for hours in the pouring rain, yet I was too much of a coward to jump. I had turned to crack, the only friend I knew of that could soothe the pain. Yet this time, it hadn't done its job. It had failed me. There was no escaping this time. My emotions were raging out of control. Coward that I was, unable to jump, I decided to try to get high again, maybe do more this time — anything to make these feelings, these thoughts, stop. I just needed to not feel.

I hit the corner and started turning tricks. Days passed, and then I was again stopped by the police. You see, I had never gone back to the honor center to do the 30 days the state had ordered. They had let me out to go to work, and my reaction had been to get off the bus and get high. So now I had a warrant due to my escape. I went to jail, and then the following morning, I went straight back to the state penitentiary.

I was off to R and O (Reception and Orientation) yet again. It was the sixth trip for me, and it would be my last.

I was greeted by an officer with, "You're back."

I remember saying in return, "Are you surprised?" I was not.

I entered the holding tank, hands cuffed, with chains around my waist and shackles on my ankles. The officer began the process of unlocking the chains. I was glad. It was a five-hour trip to the camp, and not a comfortable one, in a van with other inmates on their way to prison. After the shackles were removed, I went to the holding tank, to remove the jumpsuit that belonged to the Jackson County jail. When you're dressed out at the county jail to go to camp, you can't wear panties or a bra, or socks either. This makes the shackles on the ankles very uncomfortable, and you're grateful for your arrival at prison.

Removing my bright orange, one–piece jumpsuit and putting on a see–through gown similar to a hospital gown, I sat and waited. Concrete and steel benches hung on the wall. You just sit and wait. There's a toilet with no door, so there's no privacy. There's a large glass window so the officers can watch as you sit and await the next step.

My next step was to have my nails cut off. No long nails are allowed, so clip, clip, clip. Then the shower. I was kind of glad for that one; I had been out on the avenue for two weeks. It's a push–button shower with about thirty seconds of cold water: not a pleasant experience by any means.

There were about 20 or so of us that day, but girls came all day long to be booked in. So we were called two at a time. In this room there was cold steel and tile, with big drains in the floor. There were two stalls with showers and a window where I would get my clothing issue. I was totally naked now, standing side by side with the other people.

They began the search. Arms up...lift your breasts...run your fingers through your hair. Open your mouth...turn around...squat and cough. Lift your feet...between your toes. Spread your fingers...then spread your butt cheeks. Done.

Turn around. Raise your arms. This is the fun part. Bug spray. Yep, bug spray. It's cold and it stinks. The officer sprays your privates, your underarms. Then you bend over, and from a gallon jug, she pours ice–cold bug spray onto your head.

Cold, naked, and exposed, I heard her say, "Fifteen minutes." The timer was ticking away. We waited for the bug spray to do its bug thing. I was shivering, sleepy, and sad, yet I was feeling a kind of comfort. Shoot. It was my sixth trip. At least this was something I knew how to deal with.

At last the ding. "Time's up." Into the hot shower I went, to wash the filth and bug spray off.

I knew this would be the last time for good conditioner. They give that to you on a little piece of thin cardboard. I had long hair, and the bug junk burns your hair badly. I had learned from previous trips that I had to get the bug stuff out first and then leave the conditioner in for as long as possible if I didn't want my hair to fall out later.

The officer had returned. She had girls waiting.

"Get out!" she ordered.

So out I came. I had saved some of the conditioner to put in my hair after I got out of the shower. State issue does not include a brush, and if you want any more conditioner after that first shower, you have to buy it yourself from the $7.50 per month you earn in prison for your work there. I didn't have any money. So, to try to save my hair, I needed to get as much of this conditioner into it as possible. While the officer was giving out state–issue paperwork, I tried to clump together the conditioner that remained on the cardboard, but it dribbled off onto the floor. That was a mess, but I swiped my hand across the floor where the conditioner had run off and rubbed it in my hair.

I was still naked, but wrapped in towels. They gave me some clothes. I'm still not sure how the girls that work in clothing issue do it, but each and every trip back, whenever I and the others got out of the shower, they had a pile of bras and panties, and they always got the sizes right. I guess they have all the time from the body check to the bug spray to the showers to assess the sizes. The jumpsuit allows everyone to know you've just gotten on grounds. It's about eight sizes too large. You get boots, four pairs of socks, four pairs of panties, two bras, a towel and washcloth, a small tube of toothpaste, and a small bottle of wash for hair and body.

Oh, and the small finger toothbrush. I guess that during the time I was out, the prison decided to take away the regular toothbrush and replace it with a thimble–type thing that fits on your finger. Later I learned that several people had been injured or killed by people shaving the head of the full–sized toothbrush into a point and using it as a weapon, so no more full–sized toothbrushes in MO DOC (Missouri Department of Corrections).

Out I came, seeing others coming and going, people I had done time with. No one is allowed to speak, at least in R and O. You can't speak to the inmates already on camp. This being my sixth trip, I knew most people. I could hear the muttered voices, "She's back." I would turn and smile and say, "Yep."

Next step: We were offered a sack lunch. I had had no breakfast or lunch, and it was already afternoon, so the peanut butter sandwich was great.

We were being called one by one to the property room. This is where the clothes you had on when you were arrested are thrown away. Or you may mail them to someone if you have someone to mail them to and the money to do that. The state will pay for it, but then your first state pay is taken, and I knew I would need my $7.50. So I marked for my clothes to be thrown away.

Actually, I did have $20, but there was no way I could get to it right away. I'd been in a trick's car when the police had begun following us. The guy had picked me up a number of times before over the years, so he knew me. This time, he had paid me before we had a chance to turn a trick. Seeing the police behind us, he had just pulled over and let me out, letting me keep the money. The cops had let him drive off and arrested me. But when they take your money from you in jail, it has to come from the county later. So it would be weeks before I could use it.

Got my paperwork and returned to the lobby area. Next, pictures and prison ID. Ten sets of four pictures are taken, and then they're sent to all the offices on camp, to the visiting rooms, for FBI records, for state records, and other places I'm not sure of. You sit with your feet on the floor, facing in different directions, and you just make a three–quarter circle in a robotic pattern until the last shoot. At last she says, "Ten. This is the last set." Next, the state ID, which has to be worn at all times for all to see. DOC 1045473 is my number. It's been the same number with each trip to camp.

But this trip would be different for me, with an event to change every part of my life.

First off, this time, I was carrying a baby in prison. Second, I would be forced to make choices I had never thought I would have to make. This time, I would leave a changed person.

I was placed on suicide watch. At the time of my arrest, I had explained in tears to the officer that this was the first time I had thought of taking my own life. I had climbed over the ledge of the bridge and had stood there for hours, debating what to do. Then, being too much of a coward to jump, I had left the bridge to get high. So the prison officials decided to send me to the hole to make sure I was no longer a danger to myself or others.

I've made a few trips over the years to the hole. It's quiet, and if I had a choice of doing time in a room of four or six women or going to the hole, of course I chose to do hole time.

The white shirts approached me. "Stand up and cuff up." I placed my hands behind my back. I really was glad to go to the hole, where I would get some sleep. I had been up for three days, maybe four, and I was tired. In R and O, sleep is a hard thing to find. There are 100 females in one room, and the rules don't allow you to sleep. So I was okay with getting a couple of days to regroup.

Entering the Ad Seg (Administrative Segregation) area, I stripped and showered yet again. No bug spray this time. Then I was placed in a cell with no sheets or blankets, at least for the first day, to make sure I wasn't a danger to myself. It was the week of Thanksgiving, so many workers were off.

At last I was allowed to return to R and O, so I could be processed and placed on the grounds with the general population.

Caught up on my sleep and feeling much better, I was glad to see and be around other people. As great as the solitude of the hole can be, after 10 days of no human contact, with no sound other than the hollow slam of steel doors and the occasional screams of the women in the mental health side of Administrative Segregation, it was good to get out.

I was given prison grays and sent to R and O. Part of that is Diagnostic Orientation, which is one of the first steps of prison. That's when your custody level is determined, and a physical is given: two TB tests, an HIV test, and a hepatitis test. Your mental health and education level are evaluated. They take dental X-rays, check you for lice, and fit you for your state-issue uniforms, on which they place your name and Department of Corrections inmate number. And if you're a parole violator, as I was, they process your violation information during this time.

This time, being pregnant, I was seen by a doctor during this process. They want to make sure you're truly pregnant before they give you milk with meals. I was. They did an ultrasound. I hadn't told the doctor what I'd been told just weeks before about the baby. Maybe the tests were wrong.

However, after the exam, the prison doctor gave me a slip of paper, saying I was to be on activity restriction. Also, he was ordering tests for me at another hospital. He had some concerns about what he'd seen on the ultrasound.

As I was leaving the room, I asked, "Could you tell if it's a he or a she?"

He said he would suggest that I not get too attached to the idea of the baby at this point, until they ran more tests. I would see him again in one week.

This was in December, so I was still in the early months of the pregnancy. My heart hurt. Now what?

I went to my room in R and O. I had three roommates; they were cool. I returned to my room and cried. What the doctors on the outside had said before my return to prison must have been true. But could it change? There were still months until the baby would come.

I sat down to write Matt, my baby's father. I hadn't spoken to him in weeks. He was clean and sober, as far as I knew, so when I had decided to use again on the outside, I had stayed clear of him, so as not to bring him down, too.

I wrote to him, soon getting a letter back from him. He said that he was happy and even asked me to marry him. He had written the words in black and red marker on the outside of the envelope. When the guard called my name for mail call, I remember him laughing, announcing to the rest of the bay, "Looks like someone might be a Mrs. instead of a Miss before too long." Then he said, "So, a proposal by mail? Gals get a lot of those in letters, but this is a clear 'Let the rest of the prison know' type of marriage proposal!"

All the gals laughed and cheered. Then at count, they asked, "So what are you gonna tell him? Is it yes or no?" Those kinds of things are so exciting inside prison walls. He was reassuring me that if I was still in prison at the time of our baby's birth, he would care for him or her until my release. Oh, what comfort! I had not yet explained the concerns about the baby, and I didn't yet know enough to do this. As far as Matt was concerned, I was carrying a healthy baby, and it would be his first child.

I would write him and tell him yes to the proposal. And I would share the concerns about our unborn child.

Chapter 15

My Pregnancy with Mary Christine

Thinking back to my pregnancy with Mary Christine, I find that a lot of my memories are foggy. Much of the pregnancy consisted of sadness prior to my blindness, as I knew early on that the child I was carrying had some medical conditions that we would not know the full extent of until her birth. In addition, I knew that I had uterine fibroid tumors, with a very large one located by the placenta. It was growing as the baby grew, thus there was a large risk of brain damage to my child.

The doctors suggested that I not become attached to the baby, as they felt I would miscarry before the fourth month. However, I didn't. Then came the fifth month, and then the sixth, and soon she would be born. But it was a fight.

Just as during the early weeks after learning I was going to have a baby, I was thrilled. At last I was getting my life together. I was working, still poor, yet so excited by the idea of a baby to love and care for. No one, however, plans on having a child who is going to enter the world with medical problems. Yes, there are always risks to being pregnant, but I learned very early on of the grave concerns for this little life I was carrying. I learned that the child had the genetic condition of Pierre Robin sequence. Could I make a choice to continue to carry this child, knowing that she might not ever have a normal life? Yes, I did decide that, but it was so hard. With her father's help, I was going to do it and keep her.

However, as the weeks passed, I started bleeding. After going into pre–term labor, I was hospitalized to bed rest and medications to try to help the baby survive. As weeks passed, I could not hold down food and was very weak. At least once a week, I would go to the county hospital, as the prison infirmary/hospital was limited as to what they could do to help me. I was in labor for a couple of days, praying they could and would stop it. At last they found a medication that slowed the contractions. I was not allowed to sit up any longer or walk to the shower. They wheeled me in a bed or chair to the shower or to the phone, because every time I moved or sat up to eat, I would start having contractions all over again.

In about the fifth month, going into the sixth, I was losing weight and the baby was not growing. In fact, she was only in the 11th percentile of where she should have been regarding weight, with a healthy baby being at 100 percent. So she was a long way from that. The doctors and I decided that I would get steroid shots every four hours for five days, if I remember correctly. The shots would hopefully encourage her growth and her lungs to develop in case she was going to come early, with the contractions mostly caused from the tumor triggering the uterus.

The risk of her coming early was great, and even more so as she grew. And we prayed she would grow. I was confined to bed. I wasn't allowed to talk on the phone for more than five minutes every two weeks. I couldn't sit up to look out the window because of the large risk to me and the baby. I would rub my tummy, praying for movement.

And I would sing to her. Now I'll add that I couldn't tote a tune in a bright red bucket, so the poor child had to suffer for months of me whispering tunes and talking to her, encouraging her, telling her that she was loved.

Officers would sneak me candy bars and other treats. They brought a TV in and set it up for me. They even brought in the phone on which I was allowed to make those direct phone calls every two weeks. I gained a new view and appreciation of many prison guards I had known over the years of my incarcerations.

Then things got worse — for me, not the baby, as I learned she had put on eight ounces in a few weeks' time. It was a great start, so we were encouraged that she would pull through. I would face her conditions at birth.

I became ill, with headaches so bad I couldn't look at lights or stand the sound of even a whisper. I remember that even hearing the sheets move made me cry. The doctors came in to see me and told me I had something called uveitis. My right eye was protruding out past my brow bone. The pressure in my eye was sky high, and I couldn't see out of it. My face, head, and eye were swollen in pain. Within hours, blood had filled the right eye, and after another day, I awoke to no sight in the left eye. It had developed a rare genetic condition called VKH, Vogt–Koyanagi–Harada disease, which I would not be diagnosed with for another year, only after having seen a number of doctors.

I would also learn at that time that I had Stickler syndrome. Throughout my life, I had had unexplained pain. Once, at the age of about eight, I couldn't walk. I just couldn't do it. I know my mom thought I was faking, and after a few days, it passed. But there were other times like that, too. I also had severe knee pain during my youth, and throughout my life, I would have a great deal of pain just getting out of bed in the morning to walk across the room. After moving around for a hour or so, I could move properly.

The doctors and I agreed that during all my years on the streets, the crack probably acted as a painkiller, keeping me unaware of the chronic pain and joint deterioration I was suffering, which continue to this day.

Stickler syndrome affects the soft tissue of the body, like the eyes and ears, as well as the lower back and joints. When we learned I had Stickler syndrome, we realized that it, in combination with the VKH, is why I had such devastating results when the VKH peaked.

In darkness, unable to move, unable to bear sound for two months as the disease peaked, praying for the life of my daughter, I could have taken medications to help control the inflammation in the eyes, and they might have saved my eyes. However, the medicine was a huge risk to the child I was carrying. Thus I was faced with another choice: save my sight or the child. The baby, which I already knew to be a girl, had had a hard enough time already. I had abused my own life for years, so I made the choice to not take the medications and give this young fighter a chance.

Already knowing she had some hills to climb and not knowing how many more there would be for her after she arrived, I contacted her father to tell him. I learned that he was unable to parent our baby. *The* baby. So here I was. I had spoken to Matt only three or four times while pregnant, believing that he was going to handle the baby I was fighting to save. Now what??? Panic!!!

I knew I was to blame — not for her medical conditions, as I had been clean for almost a year before I got pregnant. But it was my fault that I had chosen the coward's way out when I learned early on of her many health concerns. It was my fault for choosing to use again and getting sent back to prison.

Now here I was in prison, carrying a child that might not live once it was born totally blind. It was a lot for anyone to handle. Matt had no car, and he had a minimum wage job. Also, the doctors had prepared us to expect that even if she did live, she would have to be hospitalized for many, many months.

Both of our hearts were breaking. I knew Matt blamed me because I had used again and had returned to prison. I blamed him because he was on the outside, and how come he could not have gotten a car by then? Torn, in turmoil, I had to make a choice, and it was clear that neither of us would be able to parent this child I had just spent months hoping would live to be born, would live to enter the world.

Oh my God, I thought, my daughter might not even live once she's born. I'm now hospitalized for my conditions, and I'm blind.

So I had to search for care for my daughter even while I was trying to figure out what was next for me. Time was short, as they were going to induce her birth so she could get the immediate care she would need to breathe and survive. So adoption was the obvious next step. After all those months of planning to be a mother, I knew I just couldn't do it — not blind, not with a baby with serious health conditions. The doctors didn't even know if she would live. So I set out to find an adoptive family, not a foster family, to look after her while I got better. I didn't want my daughter to be alone, not for one minute. If she wasn't going to make it, I wanted to know that someone who loved her would be beside her at the end.

It was an interesting journey to her adoptive parents, but I knew in my heart that the woman would love her as her own and be by her side as if she were the birth mother. She would be a mother to her, whereas I could not. We had some more rocks along the way, dealing with some folks out there who are just not very understanding of the adoption choice, who don't understand why some of us might make this choice.

Mary Christine is her name. I still remember the phone call, when they asked me if I would mind if they gave her my name. I remember saying, "Really?" I knew then that I too would be a part of this child's life — the child I had so wanted to keep and be a mother to, the child I so loved. During all those weeks and months that I spent alone in the hospital, unable to see, and for a period unable to hear, her movements in my tummy were all I had. The strength I found was from her little life growing inside me.

I was so scared, being newly blind. But I couldn't afford to break down, because any stress could trigger labor, and we couldn't risk her being born before we had lined up all the specialists she would need as soon as she entered this world, specialists who would take charge and give her the best possible chance at life. I had so bonded with this little life inside me, so deeply regretting using. But I couldn't take back the fact that I had used. Nor could I change the fact that I was there in that prison hospital, with every sound causing me pain.

I was released weeks after her birth. I was unable to see her at birth, due to their need to open her air passages so she could breathe and get a feeder tube in so she could eat. I do remember the doctor returning to my room after her birth. He said they had been prepared. They had a great team. She was connected to tubes, and she had a special mouthpiece to keep her from strangling on her tongue. I said that I was indeed lucky, as was the baby. We were lucky that we had caught her condition so early on, so they were prepared at her birth for her many special needs. He said she had a strong fighting chance to make it. Then he gripped my hand tightly for a moment and left the room.

I think it was three weeks before the doctors felt I could handle the trip to Kansas City to live with Mary Christine's birth father, Matt. After her birth, I was returned to the prison hospital from the county hospital. By then, my hearing had returned almost completely. I did suffer some slight hearing loss that was not reversible. I was able to take medications for the inflammation of the eyeballs, so at last we could stabilize my situation. And I was holding down food.

Before I had entered prison pregnant, I had gained weight during those 13 months on the outside. Eventually, I got up to 191 pounds. However, the day I left the county hospital in order to return to the prison infirmary/hospital to continue to recover, I weighed in at 153 pounds. My legs trembled when I walked during the weeks after her birth, as I was waiting to be okay to leave prison. They would walk me arm-in-arm up and down the hallway, just a few steps every couple of hours, helping me to rebuild my strength. For weeks, I longed for my little girl, and blind or not, I felt the need to fill the emptiness.

Upon leaving the prison hospital, I still had a long road ahead. I moved in with Matt, and he cared for me. I continued to need eye drops every hour on the hour, 24 hours a day. Given that I was blind and couldn't yet care for myself, he did what needed to be done, taking on cooking for me, helping me eat without making a mess, sometimes even assisting me in bathing, as I was so weak and still had a long road ahead as I tried to regain my strength from the ordeal I had just experienced. I will always be grateful for all he did for me as I transitioned to life as a newly blind person.

Yet I found myself unable to fill the void. I would often cry for hours when Matt was away at work. I was unable to simply grasp the moment. I was unable to move on from mourning the loss of giving our daughter up for adoption. I was frightened of all the sounds around me in the darkness, feeling like a prisoner in my own mind. I was obsessing, now, about how to make my heart stop hurting, how to distract myself, how to bear being in the dark, blind. The only rational thought I could muster was that of having another child to fill the void. So I decided to have another child. I told Matt what I wanted. Later, we would have a little boy and name him Ricky.

Both of our hearts were in pain, with both of us carrying blame. No one knows just what to do in situations like these. I was blind. We would attempt to save my eyesight if we possibly could, but meanwhile, we were going to have a child. We were going to parent this child, and we were going to begin our family.

Photographs of Christine McDonald

Mugshot #1

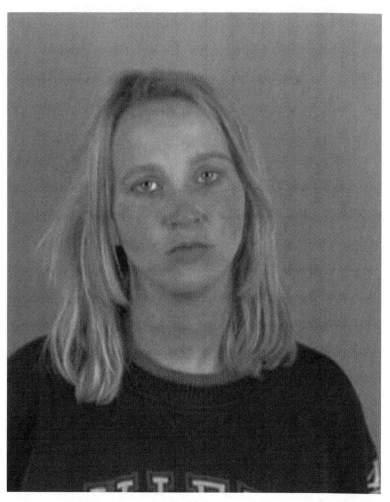

Mugshot #2

Mugshot #3

Mugshot #4

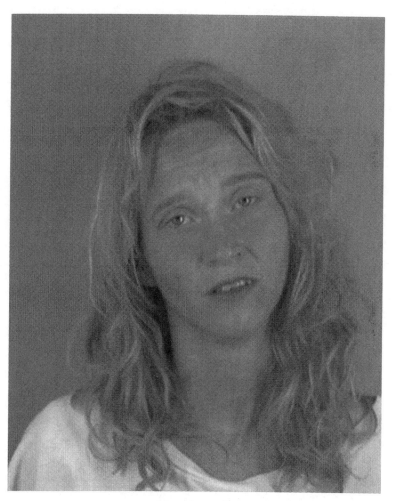

Mugshot #5

Mugshot #6

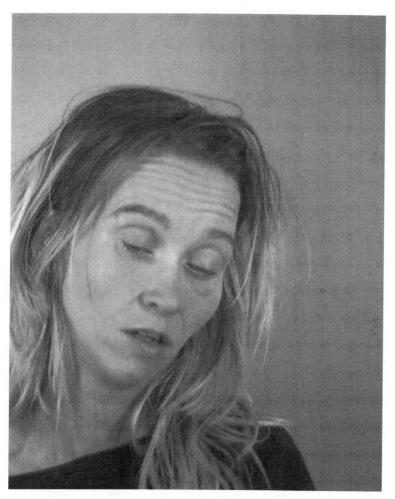

Mugshot #7

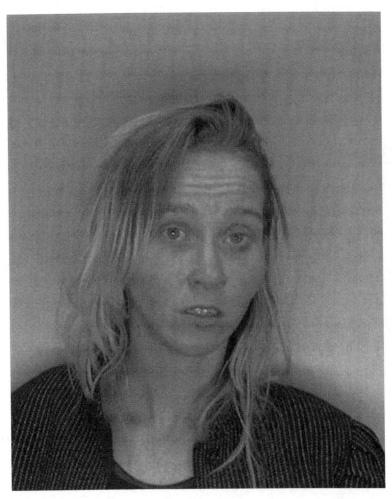

Mugshot #8

Christine at Community Employment

Christine Speaking

Christine at Home

Chapter 16

Where Is My Baby?

"Where is my baby?" I remember asking. "I want to hold my baby." He had ingested lots of blood during the delivery, so they had to suction his stomach. Seven pounds, I remember hearing. I felt so weak and tired, and it was uncomfortable in the room without sight, what with all the movement and the waiting. Ricky was crying in the background. I knew that was a good sign. He was still in the room with me, and that was also a pretty good sign that he was just fine. The nurses told Matt that he could come hold our son.

I hadn't gone to the doctor during the pregnancy, because I was fearful that something would be wrong with my baby, so I was relieved that Ricky was okay. I learned early in my pregnancy with Mary Christine that there was a problem, and remembering that always made me cry. Additionally, I was now blind, and leaving my home was hard. We had a little one–room apartment with a small kitchen and a bathroom that we shared with another apartment. It was small, but it was all we could afford. I found safety there, tucked away, rarely even stepping outside to the porch. After I lost my sight, Matt had the landlady move him to a back apartment with no stairs and a small porch for me to come out and sit on. That was very thoughtful.

I heard Matt sniffle. I knew he had felt pain after Mary Christine's birth and had hated having to give her up, with us unable to care for her medical needs. This was his chance to make things right. It was for me, too.

"Hey, what about me?" I remember asking. "Can I hold the baby, too?"

I remember the warm body on my chest. With my hands shaking, I gently touched Ricky, running my hands from one end of his body to the other. He was wrapped in blankets. Then I realized, *Oh my God, I'm blind, I'll never see my son.* Had my blindness all been a dream until then? As I touched Ricky's face, a wave of pain, fear, and panic hit me. I thought to myself, *Oh my God, what do I do now? How do I care for a baby without sight?* But I was done; any reservations I had had about ever using dope again were gone at that point. I would rest. But then what?

As they allowed Ricky to stay in my room for a while, I was scared. Thousands of questions were racing through my head.

Then it was time to feed him. I thought, Now what, where's the food? My God, where's his mouth? How will I get the bottle in it?

I knew there would be lots of trial and error, that's for sure. I hadn't yet figured out this blind living, but now, like it or not, little Ricky needed me to be his mother. I would do this for him.

Okay, I remember saying to myself, *I'll find his head first, then pick him up. Good start. Okay, should I stand or sit? What if I run into something?* This was something that I had learned was common for a blind person in an unfamiliar area.

As sweat beads dripped from my forehead, I decided to sit. Then I decided to sit on the edge of the bed and roll his little table/crib next to me. I could then stand straight up without having to move or risk tripping and landing on the little guy, then sit directly back down. I stood up, picked him up, and sat down with success. Now I had to work with the bottle. Thank goodness for those neat little bottles in the hospital that are already prepared. You just remove the cap and screw on a nipple. I didn't spill a thing!

However, now I had to find his mouth. I found the top of his head and moved my fingers down. I tried to move the bottle's nipple around to get it into his mouth, but that attempt ended up with his face covered in droplets of formula. It wasn't working. However, I had an idea. I put my finger in his mouth for him to suck and then replaced my finger with the nipple. It worked! No more mess: I had found the solution.

Then there was the smell. Oh, yes, the smell, the lovely, non–refreshing smell of a newborn baby's poop. I realized that I now needed to change my little guy's diaper; I guessed this would be the next how–to, hands–on for me. *Okay,* I thought, *find him, find his body, then the diaper. But how will I know if he's clean? How will I keep him from getting diaper rash? How will I keep from wearing the baby poop from head to toe?*

So there we were in the hospital, and I was already a nervous wreck. We were planning to go home in the morning to our small apartment. Matt had found a crib in the trash with a mattress and we had cleaned it up, mended the broken parts, and set it up in the small living area we had. I was looking forward to bringing Ricky home, and then something happened to make my heart sink

The social worker in charge of our case entered the room and asked why I had not said that I had had a baby in 2000. *Here comes my past to haunt me once again*, I thought.

In 2000, I had a trick baby, the one I named Jasmine Nicole. I got pregnant on the streets and didn't know her father, had no clue who he was. I had been raped a few times on the streets, and while I was addicted, of course, there were many times I would turn a trick for money without having the guy use protection. Sometimes tricks would offer more money to not use protection. How on earth I managed to survive the risks I took without getting HIV is a miracle.

I remember telling the lady that back then, I had nowhere to live and was strung out on crack. I had no intention of trying to keep Jasmine. I was honest about that prior pregnancy.

Because of this, however, the State was called. For one, I had had no prenatal care for Ricky. I had also used at some point in the pregnancy, and I admitted this. I knew now, though, that getting high was no longer an option for me.

Now the State would be coming to make an evaluation of me and Matt.

Oh my God, are they going to take my baby? I hurt so much, and my heart was deep in my gut. Of course, I couldn't blame them for thinking I had no business with a kid. Before, I had failed at being a mother, with both Jasmine and Mary Christine.

However, I never neglected or abused my kids — even Jasmine, the bouncing baby girl I gave birth to in 2000. I knew back then I wouldn't keep her. I knew I couldn't stay clean, and I didn't care enough for myself to stop using. Even five months into the pregnancy, I weighed only 89 pounds. So the judge did the best thing he could for my little girl. The fact is, she never would have made it without his court order for me to remain in the county jail until her birth. That was what kept me away from the dope.

After Jasmine was born, I signed the papers for the State to take her. I had no home at the time, and no one to call after her birth but the dope man and a couple of pimps. So thanks to that judge, little Jazzy, who smelled so sweet and slept in my hospital bed for the two and a half days I was with her, was given a chance at a better life. Today, I am grateful for this.

So now Matt and I had to be evaluated to determine whether we would be good parents for Ricky. When Matt came back from work, I had to tell him. I had already told him I had had a baby and had given her away because I didn't know who her father was, but I hadn't told him that she had been born in this very hospital. I told Matt that I would give him custody of Ricky if need be — that is, if the State was going to take him. My son was going home with one of us; I wanted to make sure of that.

The next day, the lady came to see us, asked many questions, and then at last stated, "You had no prenatal care except during the last month. Do you have anything at your apartment for a baby?"

For the first time in 24 hours, I felt a glimmer of hope that maybe this wasn't going to be as bad as I had feared. I explained that Matt and I had just gotten a stroller and car seat out of layaway, along with sleepers, a baby tub, and lots of bottles, and that we had a crib. She didn't need to know we couldn't afford it all and that the crib had come from the trash. We knew it would be fine because we had spent days cleaning it up and fixing it up for Ricky.

Matt's job paid only $8 an hour, and I was waiting for non-government aide. We were both convicted felons with drug-related charges, and at the time, both of us were still on parole. We couldn't get housing assistance or food stamps. We had no car, and the bus didn't go all the way to where Matt worked. So he would take it as far as it would go and then walk one and a half miles to and from the bus stop — rain, shine, sleet, or snow, just like the mailman. If he missed one day during the week, we could still pay the weekly rent, but we couldn't afford his bus fare and also food. So of course bus fare came first. Sometimes we had to budget only $10 a week for food while we were paying on Ricky's layaway items.

Then the social worker asked if I had been to treatment, so they could verify it. I told her that I hadn't been to treatment, nor was I going to NA (Narcotics Anonymous) meetings. Then I explained that I was scared to leave my apartment and that I didn't even go outside anymore. In fact, Matt had to make me leave the apartment on the days I was to meet with my parole officer. So she asked if I would go to NA meetings. I said sure. She said I could take Ricky with me, that we could go to treatment together. That way, I would have others around me to help me work through this and learn how to adjust to being a blind mother. I remember the tears running down my face. I really wanted to hug that lady, and I would have if I had been able to see her to find her.

The agreement was that I would go directly from the hospital to a women's and family treatment center. They would help me find resources in the community to figure out how to cope and be a blind mother. We soon learned that there are not many blind mothers, but we did find some resources to assist me.

So I was released from the hospital and went to treatment. They decided I didn't need to be an inpatient, and they let me and Ricky return to our small Westside apartment. We had to go to outpatient treatment five days a week so I would not be isolated and would have people around to assist me with Ricky if need be. By the time I would return home from treatment in the evening, it would be time for Matt to return home from work. I would do this daily for 30 days.

I also agreed to participate in a program called TIES, which was designed to support addicted mothers. This program provides resources and support to young mothers in recovery so the pressures of life do not overwhelm them and they can continue to grow in recovery, to move forward as a mother and a family. I believe that if more programs were geared to help with life after the NA meetings and after treatment, then the challenges of life might not be such a trigger for those still in early recovery.

Soon after we were able to go home, I began to prepare for the operation to have my right eye removed. I would have had it taken out sooner, but the anesthesia was a risk to Ricky. My eye hurt so much; it pained me just to take a few steps. Every time I would bend over or lift my Ricky, it ached terribly. Who would have thought that someone could be excited to have an eyeball taken out, knowing that once it was gone, there would never be a chance for sight? But I was.

After the first night or two of spending several minutes locating Ricky's body and suffering through the pain of lifting him, I learned that it was so much easier just to let him sleep on my chest. I could feel his every move, the beating of his little heart. I would make myself a nervous wreck every time I would hear him wiggle in his crib, not knowing what he was doing. So, for my own sanity, I kept him in our bed, snuggled on my chest. Our bed was the only furniture we had in our apartment other than Ricky's crib, and this was fine. I think I felt comfort in the smallness of the apartment.

After 17 years of homelessness, of sleeping in parks, alleyways, abandoned buildings, or whatever I could find, at least I had a place to sleep and a bathroom. Although I was now blind and longed so to see my son, I was alive, which is more than I can say for many people that walked the streets with me over the years. If blindness is my punishment for all the people I wronged, for all the hustles and for all the lies, I can still say that I am grateful to be alive.

Chapter 17

The Removal of My First Eye

I had my first eyeball removed when my son was a mere five weeks old. We would have had it taken out sooner, but it was risky during the pregnancy with my little guy, so we waited. As I said in the last chapter, who would have thought that anyone could be excited about an eyeball removal? But it was painful each time I took a step, with a wave of pain from the angry nerves, where blood had pooled and was no longer dissolving. Ricky needed feeding every two hours. I could hardly stand without tears from the pain in my face and head. We knew the removal of that eye would relieve some of that for me.

Often, Ricky spent hours on my chest, as I was unable to lift him. Someone else would have to lift him and place him in my arms, so I'd find myself just letting him lie on my chest for hours. The less I moved, the less insane I felt from the chronic pain I was enduring.

I had lost a lot of blood during the rupture of the tumor during the delivery, so we had to wait a few weeks to get my blood counts up. Matt and I had to find a daycare to enroll Ricky in. He would go to his first day of daycare when he was only five weeks old. Matt and I would take him together. This would be my first away time from Ricky. We left Ricky at daycare and got in our friend's car. Then we were dropped off at the hospital for my eye to be removed.

Now you would think that eyeball removal would

constitute a hospital stay, but not in this day and age, and for sure not for folks on Medicaid. From my own experience with it, I'll say that Medicaid is indeed a great program for many. It covers the bare necessities to sustain life, but rarely without a fight does it cover things that would enhance the quality of life. They save that stuff for folks with "real" insurance. It has covered many things for me, so I'm not running the program down by any means. But for those who think that folks really love being on Medicaid, let me tell you that it covers just the basics.

The eye was taken out in a short outpatient procedure. Our ride then picked us up. I couldn't lie down for 72 hours, as the blood might clot, and I could die. We also wanted to keep the swelling and bruising down, so I slept in the car on the way to our one–room apartment. I don't remember the ride there or even leaving the hospital. Matt picked Ricky up from his first day of daycare. The next morning, he had to return to work.

We had at last gotten a cell phone. The doctor's office called to check on me about every four hours. They had sent me home with oodles of pain medication, but I was afraid to take it.

I had just had an eyeball taken out, so I knew that with it gone, there would be no chance for me to ever see again, at least with that eye. I felt pain, great sadness, and depression, a big slam of emotions. My emotions were raging wildly, just as they do for any other new mom with a baby just five weeks old. But I also felt deep sorrow for Mary Christine. She was Matt's child. She and Ricky were only 10 months apart, yet they would not be raised together. My heart was filled with sadness from messing up, from not being able to be a parent to my daughter. I now questioned whether I could care for a newborn, our little Ricky–Doo. That was our nickname for him.

Matt got him to daycare, and I was alone and frightened. That was the first time I had been really scared, the first time I was really struck by the reality of total blindness.

My friends from the streets who were clean and sober resided in a large women's home for girls battling addiction, They showed up that morning. Matt had left the door unlocked for them. It had been less than 24 hours from the time they had removed my eye. They took me to this large home to stay, and all the girls pitched in to love me and Ricky for the five days that I was not to be alone or lie down. They spoon fed me soup. They lifted Ricky to my chest and helped me hold his bottle so I would not miss a moment of his little life. For those five days, although it was in general a dark time for me, we felt surrounded with hope and love.

Then they returned us to the apartment. I was safe to be left unattended, but not up to par as of yet, so Matt took Ricky to daycare in the mornings and brought him home on his way home from work in the evenings. It took me a few weeks to recover, but the chronic pain had at last subsided for a bit. I could walk without tears. Eye drops would continue for the remaining eye, the left one. It did not yet see total darkness. It was gray but light, a shadowy gray, if I looked up to the sun or straight into lamplight. I could at least distinguish a location in a room, or tell if it was dark or light outdoors. But that was about all I could tell. I had no measurable sight; I couldn't distinguish colors or faces. I could only tell if it was daytime or nighttime, or if a light was on, I could kind of tell where it was coming from in a room.

The inflammation in the left eye was controlled with eye drops, oodles of eye drops every couple of hours, so it had not yet reached the point of total pain. However, it was dying. I had a number of laser surgeries, something like 26, to try to allow light to peek through. They reattached the retina, which had torn when the inflammation had gotten out of control. The swelling would go down for a while, and then it would rage again. They replaced the lens of the eye to get some of the scar tissue off, to allow light through. The optic nerve was working, but the eye was dying rapidly. There were so many operations: the one to reattach the retina, then the cataract operation, and then the laser treatments every few weeks. All that enabled me to see lights and wavy images of objects, but I was unable to clearly identify any objects. However, as I said, I could tell where a window or a light was. That kind of helped me get a idea of where I was in a room.

The laser treatments allowed the light to seep in a bit, at least for a little while. After each treatment, I would rush around the house, looking up at the lights or opening a curtain at a window to let the light in. There was no darkness, at least for a few days, anyway. But the light would dim slowly by the end of a week's time. By then, the abnormal cells would have collected to the point where no light could penetrate. My doctor said that there might come a time when the lasers could no longer work, a time when the eye would be too weak for him to use the lasers any longer.

And that time did indeed come: total darkness. So there I was, with a baby and living in total darkness — missing the chance to see my baby's first smile, unable to see his first everything, unable to see the sparkle of newness in everything a small child embarks upon or encounters.

I kept thinking that there had to be something out there, that there had to be some chance for me to see again. I had so many wrongs to right, so much seeing left to do. Sometimes people do not realize the hugeness of what I mean when I say that I just don't know much about a particular thing, because I've never seen it. They remind me that I've only been blind for six years, seven as of this March. At that point, I have to remind them that I spent 17 years on the streets and in prison, unable to go to a Walmart or a grocery store. In my present life, I have many firsts, many discoveries. Because I was an addict from such a young age, so out of it so much of the time, many times now I am much like a young teen just embarking on life.

Chapter 18

Our First Rental Place

What excitement! Matt, Ricky, and I were going to move from our one-room apartment to a house, a small rental on the northeast side of Kansas City. The place was old, but living in a one-room apartment and sharing a bathroom with the occupants of another apartment was no longer really working for us.

I was thrilled. My friends helped us clean the little rental up. It was a mere few blocks from the avenue where I had existed in addiction for years, and that was scary. I often worried that people from the avenue would see me. I myself was no longer able to see, and I had already had one eyeball removed. I was scared that someone from my past might see me, someone I had done wrong. I was clean. I didn't miss that life, didn't miss the drugs. I was still scared, though.

However, I was committed to Matt and to our son. I was committed to doing the next things in life, the right things. Ricky was just a few months old. And now, being blind, I knew that I was unable to protect us.

Given that Matt and I were both convicted drug felons, we really struggled to find a place. My long arrest history, my numerous felonies, and our limited income were all barriers. At the time, we were both on parole. Matt still didn't have a car, so he was taking the bus to take Ricky to daycare, then taking the bus to work. I was using public transportation for the disabled, working in a sheltered workshop half the day, then spending the rest of the day learning to live blind. Matt picked Ricky up from daycare and then returned home.

When we finally found a landlord willing to rent to us, he raised the rent by $100 a month due to our criminal backgrounds and our having no rental history. Then he demanded that we sign a five–year lease. Matt and I signed. We had been struggling so hard to find a place, but had kept being turned down. We wanted a better place than this for our son. We wanted a better part of town. But with our backgrounds, the bad side of town and renting from a slumlord were our only options. Those are the only places that are willing to take you if you have a criminal background. Yet I longed in my heart for a better life for little Ricky. I still believed in the American Dream, was still praying that we would not always be judged by our mistakes — for Ricky's sake.

So we moved to the little place, and my friends helped us get a few starter items for it from the thrift store. Soon afterwards, we had a visitor.

Someone was knocking at the door. I was scared to open it, but then I heard a woman say, "Hello! I'm Kris, from the church down the street." I guess she could see me inside the house, as we were not done hanging curtains. Sometimes I have to remember that just because I can't see, it doesn't mean that others can't see me!

I opened the door and let her in, and we visited. She invited us to church. It was just down the street, on the corner. I agreed. For sure, this was what I needed to continue on my path of growth, away from the streets!

Attending the church, I realized that it was located right across from my favorite corner, the one where I had worked for years, at Spruce and Independence Avenue. There were three churches there, one right on the corner. That one used to run me off all the time, or someone there would call the police if I was outside the church. The other one was on the hill across the street; it always had police parked in the parking lot ready to run me off.

Then there was this little church. It was very small, kind of like a little house, behind Sonic. I had slept in its doorway before, gotten high in the parking lot. I think I had even been invited in for service one year by someone who was going into the church on a Sunday morning. At the time, I was walking to the corner to work, returning from a dope house. I had of course kept walking.

Now here I sat inside that same church. I asked someone, wanting to make sure I was correct in my thinking about where it was. I was.

Feeling a connection, feeling drawn to attend, I joined that little church and got baptized. When I was taken out of the baptism water, I asked, while wiping the water away, in front of the congregation, "Can I join your outreach team now?"

You see, I had a dream. I had a vision of something pulling at my heart strings. But I knew I couldn't do it alone.

They agreed, and I started attending the meetings. I sat in a meeting listening to their plans to reach out to the community. At last I had a moment to speak. I asked, "What about the homeless addicts and prostitutes who exist outside here, along this street?"

I told them that when we're in addiction, it totally governs our thoughts. We don't think about spending money on food. It isn't on purpose; it's like bondage. You mean to buy food, but then you think about what you did for that money, and it's easier to get high, to wash away that thought, the guilt and shame. You're fighting off the emotions with drugs, rather than food.

It was a go. We started Brown Bag Fridays. We took sandwiches, sometimes burritos, and sometimes $1 double cheeseburgers. We would drive up and down the streets of the area and ask if they were hungry. Rarely did anyone say no! But in that case, we would say, "You can always save it for later," and they would take it.

We expanded, collecting coats and jackets and socks. We would go out on Christmas Eve and pass out goodie bags, also food. On Thanksgiving, we would put together a hot Thanksgiving meal and then drive up and down the streets, giving out hot meals.

This was my passion, my calling. I knew it. I knew in my heart that these folks needed us, that they would at least eat when we came through.

I would often meet up with my friends, the people I had co-existed with on the streets. My journey on the streets, through all those years, had given me an understanding of their lifestyle, an empathy, an understanding of their needs. I had walked in their shoes and had survived. Now I was filling a need, helping these people to not feel invisible, the way I had all those years, often wishing, even praying, for someone to pull up beside me and hand me food, with no strings attached — not having to be preached at, not having to be turned away due to having no shoes.

Now I had this huge passion for acceptance, for acceptance of those people right where they were.

Now my life was starting to become full. I was a new mom. I was also continuing to learn to live blind, becoming less scared as each week passed in my rehabilitation training. And now, with this new passion for community outreach, I was giving back, offering hope to those with none.

However, I was still longing to see. I would pray: If I could see, I could be such a better mom, and think of how many other things I could do to help those in so much pain on the streets! I knew their pain, and I had experienced the joy of leaving the streets, of being in love, and being a mom. I wanted safety for my friends. It was not always easy, but I thought that if they kept seeing me out there, trying so hard to help them, then they would have hope that they could also leave that life on the streets.

I was still struggling, though, with trusting. I really had no trust for anyone other than Matt. My lack of trust, which was left over from my former life, was something that would take a long time to heal from.

I had a family advocate at Ricky's daycare, someone who took a huge interest in our lives. She saw my struggle to do right, saw how I was recovering from addiction and life on the streets, trying to learn to be a blind mom and also trying to figure out how to be a good mom.

She reached out to the media about our rent price being so high and about the outrage of a five-year lease, about my working in a sheltered workshop and my never having a chance to see my child. The community responded. One family who was dealing with a battle against cancer offered us their family Christmas tree; they are still our friends today. Another person offered funding to find me a doctor outside of Medicaid, to see if there was anything that could be done to try to save my sight.

Then the doors opened. I had hope again. I had found hope in humanity. I had renewed hope for sight. By that time, Ricky was six months old.

We would visit a doctor hundreds of miles away to see if a new, experimental device might be the thing to maybe restore the sight in my remaining eye, the left one. Another landlord had a house for rent for far less money, which was much more within our means, and it required only a one-year lease. To our joy, he agreed to take a chance on us. Others stepped in to get us out of the five-year lease. So we moved again, but this time, it was to a place we could afford. It was still a small place, and still in the area where I had lived on the streets, but it was many blocks from the drug-infested strip we had been living by.

Meanwhile, I had a visit from my parole officer. At last I was done! I had walked down my last nearly two years of parole on the outside. I mainly have Matt to thank for that. He ensured that I got to my meetings. He took care of me.

I have a great deal to thank Matt for. He took care of me in my despair when I was newly blind, unable to get from one room to the next, needing someone to check if I was leaking during my period, cooking for me, ensuring I got all my eye drops, putting ointments in my eye socket and eye, changing my bandages after each surgery, sometimes even having to bathe me. Often he took on many extra responsibilities with Ricky. And for all those things, I will always be truly grateful.

Chapter 19

A Glimmer of Hope

I had a glimmer of hope at one point. When Ricky was almost one year old, I learned of an implant that might allow the pressure in my left eye to elevate enough that we could replace the lens of the eye once again. I was so hopeful! This was a new device, and the operation was costly.

We made the trip to meet with a team of doctors, to see if this might be the thing for me. After they examined me, I was excited, but the silence in the room was deafening. So I broke it. "Well? Can we try?"

They agreed we would give it a try. Now to get the insurance company to cover it. As I said before, I had Medicaid — not the greatest and not the worst, but I was told by the doctor's office that they had attempted to get this for another patient and had been denied. I felt a grumble in my stomach and responded, "Well, the other eye has been removed. This is the only chance I have."

I was first told that because the other eye had been removed, the law said that we must preserve the remaining eyeball, and the operation was too risky. I pleaded with them. "I just want a chance to see my son Ricky and my daughter Mary Christine, even if only for a few minutes. Please, just a few minutes of sight!"

They said we would proceed. Now to contact the insurance company. The doctor had to submit his request and justify us risking my remaining eye. The operation was approved, but not the implant; they denied payment of the fee for the device. We contacted the hospital to see if we could get the device at their cost. We could, but then my doctor went one step further. He went to the company that made the device and explained my story.

We waited. Time moved so slowly! I knew, just as the doctors did, that every day, every hour that passed, my chance of getting the implant lessened because of the growth of scar tissue and abnormal cells. The pressure in the remaining eyeball was so low that there to continued to be a greater and greater risk that more cells would die.

At last it was a go. The company that made the device said yes, they would donate the device for me for free. There was just one more thing we needed to do. Time was passing, and the risks grew higher. I was a wreck. This was a chance, a chance to come out of the darkness, a chance to see my little Ricky for the first time, a chance to see the world as a clean and sober person, a chance for me to be a full and complete mom. But the company needed a letter from the insurance company stating that they did not cover the implant.

I was on it. I called Medicaid. I called and called. Who was I to get this from? I had the doctor fax a request. We waited some more. At last, there it was in the printer. The phone had rung. It was a fax. I scanned it into the computer to allow my screen reader to read it. I assumed this was the letter I needed. We could book the operation, and maybe I would have the hope for sight. I cried. With my heart pounding, I called the doctor's office. "I got the letter," I said. "Get to booking my operation!"

Then my computer came on. It began reading the letter. I was so happy, and then it happened. The device, the implant, was not covered because it was a "Dental Implant." Yes, that's how Medicaid had classified the implant, and Medicaid does not cover any dental procedures for adults. But this was an optic implant, not a dental implant. How could Medicaid make such a mistake in classification?

I got off the phone. I had to start the computer over to reread the letter. I went through the records I kept on the computer, then called the hospital. I had to confirm the device number. They were one and the same. I called the doctor. "The device is denied because it's for a dental procedure, and such devices are only covered for children and in emergencies for pregnant females."

He couldn't believe it. I faxed it to his office. He sent it to the company that made the device, saying this would not work. They needed the device to be correctly classed as an ocular implant in order to be able to donate it. So it was back to the drawing board. Then we got a doctor at Medicaid. We sent my records reports on the implant and prayed.

Two weeks passed. I got a call. It was the hospital. Medicaid had corrected the mistake in the system and they were going to cover the implant as well as the operation. In the course of this wait, nearly four months had passed. We didn't have a lot of hope of success left, but we were going to give it a try anyway.

Just before the surgery, I was informed that my eye could collapse during the operation, as there was no pressure. We prayed. I had IV and med lines in me. I was ready to go. I reminded the doctor, "Hey, I'm only hoping for a few minutes of sight." I told everyone to have my babies ready for me to see.

I remember waking up in a hotel bed. I guess after the operation, they had wheeled me to the hotel in the hospital to rest. I remember saying to Matt, "I don't know if I can see yet." He was silent. He and my friend Malcolm, a reporter, said we would talk to the doctors in the morning. They knew the results.

I went to see the doctor. He was kind and thoughtful. He said he had spent four and a half hours trying to remove scar tissue, but it had grown into the cellular body of the eye and he could not risk removing it, as the eye would surely die. He was sorry.

We gave it a try. We removed the patch. I could tell there was a light near my eye. It hurt badly. It had been so long since the last time I had seen a light that it was painful. The doctor replaced the patch and said, "We'll see."

Over the next couple of weeks, the pressure did not rise, and the bright light I had seen at the doctor's office disappeared, never allowing me to see the faces of my son or daughter.

Darkness.

Chapter 20

Stem Cells: My Last Chance

I was now in tears, because the device we had fought for me to get had not worked. I crashed into depression for a few days, and then shook it off. After all, I still had one eye, even if it didn't see. Although the right one had been removed, I still had my left eye. While I was at the hospital, they had tested the optic nerve, and it was still working. My only hope now was to save the non–seeing eyeball until science or technology could come up with a way to restore my sight.

I received a call from the doctor who had fought with me to get the implant approved by Medicaid. He told me that due to my getting the classification of the device changed, three people had had their sight saved in a timely fashion. My thought then was that at least *something* good had come out of all that despair!

Preserving my non–seeing eye was all I could think about, knowing that the one thing that had given us hope had failed. I was devastated, crushed, dreaming about sight, about seeing my child for the first time. I had been clean, now, for nearly two years, and I was in college. My heart had grown so much with being a mom, and I was longing to see my child. I felt a great drive to find a way to save my left eye, which was dying quickly.

I spent almost every waking hour on the computer, researching nutritional oddities that might save the eye or make it healthier. I was also doing a research project in college on stem cells, covering all the controversial components of the subject, the different types of stem cells, and all the promise many researchers saw in stem cell research.

I had first explored eyeball transplants and had contacted many facilities, both in our country and outside the U.S. I had learned that in some less–developed countries, research guidelines were often more lax, so the surgery might be more dangerous, but those researchers were also more willing to take risks than most American researchers were. I was fighting for my last chance to save my remaining eyeball, knowing that once it was removed, I would never see again.

Never, ever would I have a chance to see the blue of the sky that I had taken for granted for so long. I would never have the chance to see my son grow up, never have the chance to see my daughter, Mary Christine, the child I had put up for adoption. As I explained before, I could have taken medication to save my sight while I was pregnant with her, but it would have been dangerous to her. I had planned to parent her, but at the time, I was struggling hard just to learn to live without drugs. Now we have play dates with her as often as we can, so that Ricky and Mary Christine can grow up as brother and sister, knowing they are both loved and are part of each other's lives.

I learned that while parts of the eye can be replaced, the entire eyeball can't be transplanted, even in another country. Regenerating the optic nerve is the barrier.

However, during my research, I learned about something else: stem cell research, which, at the time, was not allowed in the United States. However, researchers in many other countries were testing the waters of various therapies using stem cells.

I contacted many stem cell facilities in 16 different countries, seeking someplace willing to take a chance on me. I needed to see if I could find a way, any way, to save this last, dying eye. I felt that need in the core of my being. I simply had to make one last try to preserve the eye, even if the attempt failed. I needed to at least try, so I could have the peace of knowing that I had tried everything I possibly could.

One place after another that I contacted turned me down, but at last I found a place that accepted me! They spoke of having promising results in some areas by just pumping stem cells into people. The little stem cells go in and reproduce the damaged cells. I knew it was a long shot, and they made no promises. I was content with that. At least I would have tried everything I could.

Now to raise the funds to make it happen. I was aware that I might go and it might not work. I was aware that stem cells were totally in a testing stage. I was aware that I would be heading to a third–world country and be taking huge risks. But they were risks I had to take.

I felt that I needed to see to be a full mom. I so longed to see my son! My heart was full of sorrow from longing to see his face. I was thinking of our future, of his attending school, of how I wanted to be able to help him with homework, to cheer him on in everything he did.

The community came together to help, offering funds and airline tickets. Mary Christine's adoptive parents headed up a fundraising drive to assist in the project.

Then, just a couple of weeks before it was time for me to leave, Mary Christine's adoptive parents made it clear that they felt that the clinic and stem cells were too much of a risk. Some people were claiming that stem cells worked, and others were claiming that they didn't. I knew this was a fledgling project, territory that was not yet fully explored. I fully knew all of this, but I didn't care. Yes, stem cells were still in the beginning stage, not yet developed or harnessed, but my time was running out. I couldn't wait for research to give me something definite. However, my daughter's adoptive parents felt that the clinic that had approved me was a scam, and that the risks were too great.

So they chose to retract the funds and not support the project.

I was in despair. I cried for days, torn. We allowed everyone to take their funds back.

A couple of months later, the left eye had dropped in pressure. It had lost its electric pulses in the optic nerve, and it had to be removed. Words cannot express the devastation I felt, having been in survival mode for so long, fighting so hard for my only chance to perhaps save the eye. Now all my efforts had been for nothing.

Some generous people allowed us to keep the money they had donated, so we put it in a small savings account. After most of the donors had taken their money back, we still had $4,000 left, and we bought a small trailer for that amount. It had no floors, no sinks, and no toilet, but it was ours. It had a fenced yard and a place for a washer and dryer. Matt worked to fix it up. He and some of my church friends and our dear friends, the couple that had given us their family Christmas tree, helped put fixtures in, clean the place up, and paint it. Some people from the community college I was attending came to our home and built us a little porch with stairs.

It was not much, but it was ours!

Chapter 21

Blindness and How It Has Affected Me

When I first became blind, I longed for being able to primp in the mirror, and I still miss that. And then there was struggling to learn to cope with "that time of the month." When you're blind, how do you know exactly when it starts and when it ends? There were so many things that I used to take for granted. There were all those years I wasted away, addicted and controlled by crack, unable to gather the strength to find self-esteem.

Now, finding humility, I have to ask to find the restroom whenever I go out.

A few months into rehabilitation, when I was still learning to live blind, I was given the task to go to a store and buy a item. I had to take public transportation, get inside the store, and find the item. Given that I was totally blind, I would need to rely on people around me and solicit assistance. I remember how my heart was pounding as I set out.

For months after I lost my sight, I refused to leave our small apartment. But then Ricky was born, and he needed me to learn to live blind. Often, he was the one who gave me the strength to face the fearful things I found now as a person without sight.

I asked the bus driver where the Family Dollar store was and if he could announce it so I could get off the bus at the right stop. This alone was a difficult task for me. During all those years in addiction, I had had no fear of asking for anything. But now, without sight, without drugs, and in my right mind, even these simple tasks were quite painful and hard for me. Always before, when I could see, I had been able to find my way around. But now, with little trust in anyone or anything, I was forced to trust total strangers.

The bus driver announced the store, and I stepped off. Now where was the store? Where was the door? Listening to my surroundings as I had been taught, I stopped and turned my head in the direction of some people I heard speaking.

"Excuse me," I said. "Could you please direct me to the Family Dollar store?" No one responded. I struggled to drum up the courage to ask again. There I was, the woman who had been able to find a trick, to pull off a hustle, and now I was simply trying to find a door.

I tried again. "Excuse me. I'm blind, and I want to go to the Family Dollar store. Could you please tell me what direction it's in?" I was thinking to myself, *Gosh, I hope this is not a 'hood like where I come from. I could be mugged!* I was feeling so vulnerable, almost naked, as I announced my blindness. I felt a weird, new sense of humility having to ask for help with something that would have seemed so very simple to me before I lost my sight.

At last I was directed to the store, and the man opened the door for me. "It's open," he said.

"Thanks," I said.

I moved forward. Now what? I listened for the cash register. When I heard it, I moved onward, with my white cane swaying from side to side across the floor, which let me know that the floor in front of me was clear to step.

I stopped and asked, "Where are the batteries?" A lady responded quickly, "Over there."

I thought to myself, *Here we go again!* I asked again, holding up my cane. "Excuse me, but I'm blind. I'd like to buy some batteries. Could you help?"

"I'm sorry," she said. "Please forgive me. They're right over there."

I was feeling puzzled and annoyed by her lack of common sense. So I repeated myself. "Which way is that way? To my left or to my right?"

"They're that way!" she responded. All I could guess was that she was pointing in one direction or another. But by this time, I was so disgusted that I left without my batteries, pondering how I had been disconnected from society for all those years I had spent as an addict, as a homeless person, and now I was struggling so hard, in this new way, to find my place as a blind person, to be treated as an equal to others.

It did get easier after that. The more often I had to ask for help, the easier it became, but I'll admit that sometimes it's still hard. However, I knew that I had to survive, and learning to ask for help, learning to trust total strangers for almost everything, was a huge lesson for me.

Further on in my rehabilitation, I remember sitting with a woman named Cathy. After first losing my sight, I found her to be a veteran, at least in comparison to me, in the field of blindness. She had lost her sight about 10 years prior to our meeting.

I asked her many questions, such as how we blind people dress ourselves so we don't look crazy when we go out in public. I also wanted to know if I could ever wear makeup again now that I was blind. She laughingly told me about a neat little device that I still use today, the talking color detector. It uses infrared beams to tell what color an item is, and it can even list multiple colors if more than one color is in an item. Even cooler than that is the fact that it has a male voice with a wonderful British accent. Ha, ha! What could be better than a pleasant-sounding male voice with a great British accent telling me what color my bra is every morning as I get ready to dress for the day?

I called Cathy on the phone and we talked about makeup. She said, "Just do it!" She explained about holding the mascara brush up by my eyelashes and blinking until I felt the lashes touching the brush. Trying to put on lipstick, I stopped thinking so much and just did it.

But I had to ask. "Hey, Cathy, I'm blind and can't look in a mirror. How do I know I don't have stuff all over my face?" She said, in such a cheerful, positive voice, "You did great. I'm sure you look beautiful. Just trust yourself and your abilities!"

So I did, and now I put makeup on every day before I leave the house. And guess what? I've never yet had a single person tell me that I've made a mess of myself. Now I've not only mastered putting on makeup blind, but I can even put it on in a moving car when I'm running late. Shoot, I couldn't do that without making a mess when I was sighted!

However, buying makeup and those types of items is not so easy. My trusty color detector can't tell me which shade of makeup or lipstick I need, so I have come up with another way that works for me. I go to the makeup counter and simply ask for assistance. Sometimes the tone of the clerk's voice makes me feel that she wouldn't be all that good at such a thing. Sometimes the clerk sounds either too old or too young. Anyway, I explain that I'm blind, in case they haven't figured that part out yet, and ask for them to assist me in finding reasonable prices and good colors.

Now I will also explain that I do this at Walmart and Walgreens. I can't afford the makeup at the special counters in fancy department stores, like Macy's, where they're paid to help you with this kind of stuff. I will admit I've worn some of the colors picked out by total strangers, and from what I've been told, I honestly think it's much better to take a trusted friend with you when making this type of selection.

I've done this type of thing with hair color, as well, saying to a stranger in an aisle, "I'm totally blind, and I'm looking to change my hair color. What color do you think would look good?" Then I'm so bold as to purchase the suggested color and do the process myself. I'm sure I sometimes miss sections of my hair, but overall, I think I do just fine, and I value the independence of doing it myself. I've been told that my hair color is rather different. If you also need help choosing hair colors, I recommend that you take along someone that likes you and you trust, particularly if you have plans for going out in public. It's one thing to have someone pick out a crazy, uncool shade of lipstick, but it's quite another to have someone pick out a wild, ungodly color of hair dye. Believe me, I know from experience that once the color is on your hair, a bad dye job can be pretty hard to correct. But I will also say that it's kind of fun — in a weird kind of way.

Being blind has brought me lots of unnerving thoughts about things that people who have been blind all their lives have to contend with. I find many things bothersome, like when I want to pay for an item in a store and hand over my bank card, and the cashier tells the sighted person with me, "Oh, she'll have to sign." Of course I jump in and say, "I'm only blind. I can sign. Just put my hand down where you want the signature."

It's very hard to adjust to being blind after you've spent your whole prior life being sighted. For example, when you go out to eat, the waiter or waitress will usually ask the sighted person with you, "What would she like to drink?" That always seems to start things off on a bad foot. Of course I answer, "Diet Dr. Pepper." That's my favorite. But then the server returns with the drinks and asks my sighted companion, "And what would she like to eat tonight?" Once again, I state my order, just jumping in there. Then when the ticket comes, I pull out the money and leave a tip, and the waitress still gives any change to the sighted person, saying, "Here's her change," although I'm the one who gave her the money. It's crazy.

To me, it's also degrading, almost as though they're discounting me as an individual. Often I just want to shout, "I'm only blind! That's all!" But the same thing happens over and over, time and time again. Some of my blind friends seem okay with this. Many of them have been blind their whole lives, so they're really used to this kind of thing.

But I knew life when it was different for me. Even when I was strung out, twitching and slinging my arms around, in effect saying, "Stay away," even when I was eager for that next hit, when I knew the store clerk had just seen me stand outside the store on the corner and get in a trick's car, then jump out in their parking lot and come inside to get change to call the dope man or to buy a lighter so I could feed my habit, even when I was dirty and smelly and delirious with lack of sleep — even then, no one asked the guy that might have been with me, the person who might have been cleaner, the one who was driving the car, what I wanted to buy. They still took my money and gave me the change — that is, if they hadn't decided to call the cops just because I had entered the store. And believe me, there had been more than one such call made.

Today, I am still an individual. I still have money, and I can still make purchases. So please, all you sighted clerks and waiters and waitresses — please recognize me for what I am: an individual, a thinking human being who can make my own choices, and pay with my own money, and accept my own change.

Chapter 22

Sheltered Workshop, College Entrance, and a Song for My Homeless Days

I want to share a bit about my first job while blind.

I had an 8th-grade education. I had been on the streets, addicted, for 17 years, and was now totally blind. I worked in a sheltered workshop for developmentally disabled folks who were also blind. I did what they called piece work, putting little plastic plugs into the ends of ink pens for about $6.00 per 1,000 pens. How repetitive, how boring! In my head, all I could think was, *I've stolen cars. I've sold dope to support my habit. I've survived the streets and prison. Yet this is how mainstream society views me, as developmentally disabled and blind.*

Many of the folks that worked in the workshop where I was placed valued their jobs, valued making their 20 or 30 dollars every two weeks. Some of them had job coaches. Some were both deaf and blind. Some needed help eating or going to the bathroom. Some had very childlike views of the world. Some were unable to grasp the wholeness of the world. It was a hard place to be. It made me sad.

But one thing I did know. That is, whether my lack of education was messing up my life or not, I was a mother. I did not live in a institution. I had a home. I cooked my own food. I dressed myself. And I knew that this was not at all where I belonged.

They began testing me to see if I had the ability to learn. Now how crazy was that! I knew how to hustle. You had to be a quick thinker to do that for so many years. They had to see if I could read and understand the language of communication. I took an IQ test. I took an aptitude test. I took classes to see if I could retain what I heard in a class. I had never touched a computer. I had never touched a typewriter. So, obviously, I must have had the ability to learn, as here I am writing my own book. On a computer.

I did my best to remain cool about the whole thing. I knew I could learn, or at least I thought I could learn. I had been a D student in school, so maybe I did have a learning disability. My mother had always told me I was mentally retarded. Maybe it was true, and these people knew that, and that was why I was being tested.

After the tests, I would return home to hold my Ricky with all my might, believing that I could do something with myself. I just didn't know exactly what.

I was terrified of the idea that maybe my mother had been right all the years she had told me I was retarded. After all the drugs I had fed my body, I was sure I had killed some brain cells along the way. I read about that in drug classes. Had they re-grown themselves? Was that possible?

Meanwhile, Cathy from the blind group had sent a guy named Reggie to my house to install a talking typing program. He showed me how to turn it on and practice typing. Without a GED or anything, and now blind, I knew that the computer would be my only hope of keeping in contact with the world.

I *was* able to learn. In fact, it turned out that I was a fast learner. I learned that I had a high aptitude for business, an above-average IQ, and a knack for all the computer stuff. So I would take business office classes, learn to use the computer to type, then work towards a GED.

I completed my training, then decided I wanted to be a

receptionist. So I thought I would go to business school. I took the entrance exam and passed, but I really did not want to be a receptionist, so I asked about college. Could I do that? I had just learned that I had an above–average IQ, and for the first time in my life, I knew I was not retarded. I could do whatever I wanted, become anyone I wanted. But could I actually go to college?

I would give the local college a call and see. I explained that I had no GED and had only completed the 8th grade, but that I wanted to take the entrance exam to see what kinds of classes I would need to take to get into college. I got set and went. The reader read me the questions and I answered. I was a wreck, shaking and sweating from all the pressure. The test was timed, and that made it even worse. Then I was done.

The reader left the room. It seemed like hours had passed before she returned and said, "Congratulations!" I asked why. Well, I had scored a 96% and an 86% on the tests, so I would be able to jump right in on a college level. No remedial classes needed. She said I could not get a degree without a GED or a high school diploma, but I could enter college as a freshman. And that I did.

***

My first semester was interesting. I went to class and found that I had been appointed a scribe. She and I would arrive at class together. I would have her to take written notes for me. Okay. Again, I knew I wasn't the brightest light in the yard, but I certainly knew I was totally blind. She was writing my notes, but how was I to read them? Better yet, throughout our first day, she kept asking me what I wanted her to write and how to spell stuff. I was very annoyed. I couldn't read her handwritten notes anyway, so those would serve no purpose. So I decided, newly blind and all, that I was going to do this myself. I asked her to not come with me to class anymore. My goodness, if I was going to be able to pay attention in class, I could not be distracted by her questions about what to write and how to spell words!

I was overwhelmed. My English teacher had all these requirements. Although he seemed nice, I could tell right off that I was going to be consumed with work, with research, and with trying to keep up.

After a couple of days, I contacted the instructor to say that I didn't think I was ready for his class. I had spoken to other students and knew there were easier teachers on campus, but I also knew I needed this class to continue in many of the classes I was taking in order to learn to teach others about addiction.

The instructor asked me to give it a try. "Just do a paper or two," he said. He assured me I could drop the class if he and I both felt I couldn't handle it.

The first paper broke all the ice. It related to music, and in it, we were introducing ourselves to him and the class. After getting this assignment, my very first college paper, I realized that I had hardly ever listened to music, at least not in a long time. I had been homeless. There was no electricity in the parks where I had slept, and after getting clean, I hadn't listened to music because it reminded me of being sighted. Writing the paper, I was torn and a emotional wreck, but I did it, and I made an A. Here is what I wrote.

"A Song for My Homeless Days"

Wow, what a challenge for me, after almost two decades of homelessness: not the type of homelessness where one is in an institution, a shelter, with a bed, warmth to protect you from the cold, food to still the hunger pangs, and safety from the darkness and all that lurks in it. Electricity was not readily at hand, at least not for me. So for many years, there was emptiness, with society growing and me standing still.

A song I could relate to was difficult to find. Even after I went blind, I found it hard to listen to music, remembering past experiences during my sighted life — mostly harsh, cold, painful memories, but they were sighted memories nonetheless. Yet I am determined to make this class work, to prove to myself and the world that there can always be a brighter tomorrow — no matter how bad your life is, no matter how poor your choices, and no matter how long this experience has endured in your life.

Humming tunes while cleaning my house, picking up after an 18-month-old, as a single, blind mother with no one sighted in my life, I think I found a song that says a lot about my life, at least a past part of it. The song is "I'm With You" ("Those Damn, Cold Nights"), by Avril Lavigne.

I remember the bitter cold winter wind. I was curled up, with no shoes or coat, bare legged, in a skirt, too tired to get up from the spot I had found beside a cold brick building, alone. There was no one bugging me, no one wanting anything from me that I was not willing to give. Just rest, sleep, a friendly word, a rescuer would be nice. "Could someone find me?"

The concrete so damp, the cold causing my frail body of 88 pounds to ache. Yet with my head against a vent, where part of my body found warmth, there was the brisk aroma of ground coffee beans to bring me comfort of sorts. But it was occasionally overpowered by the stale, musty smell of urine, reminding me of my reality.

In this song, I hear an insistent cry, almost a demand: "Don't know who you are, but I am with you, I am with you." I have felt this, just needing to belong, not caring to whom or what. "Isn't anyone trying to find me? Won't someone please take me home?" As I hear this, I am almost reliving the desperation, wanting a kind person, someone not wanting me as an object, a thing, but just allowing me to belong, to keep me safe, warm, to see me as a person. As I think of this, I must remember that to me, the men, too, were faceless and nameless, just there for me for a little while, as I was for them.

Today I cherish and even savor my humble house, where I have a bed to sleep, safety from the weather and from people. Hearing this song, I will not forget how far I have come, once even being considered "too far gone." Today, I sit with much gratitude and humility and feel it is a privilege to be in school.

Chapter 23

Ricky

Being a mom is something that fills our minds with insecurities even when we're able–bodied. But there I sat, blind and a mom to a sighted little boy. My mind raced all the time, always questioning my abilities to parent him.

When he was a newborn, he would lie on my chest a lot, so I could be sure not to miss what might be going on. But as he grew and learned to wiggle and move around more, I faced new levels of concerns as I tried to figure out his needs whenever he cried. I tried hard to listen to the *way* he cried, to the different tones.

I remember one time when he and I were alone, and he was crying. I changed his diaper, I held him, and I sang to him. At that time, he still sucked on his binky (his pacifier), and I offered that to him as well. No luck. We sat together on the floor, with Ricky still crying. At last I began to cry, too, as I hugged him and held him close. I remember rocking him, saying, "I'm sorry, but I just don't know what you need or want! If only you could talk!"

Then he struggled out of my arms. I let him go. Still fussing, he returned in a few moments. He grabbed my hand and placed a sippy cup in it. Here he was, not even walking yet, just crawling, yet he had brought me his sippy cup.

I gasped. "A drink?" I exclaimed. "You want a drink?"

I filled the cup, sat back down on the floor with him, and gave him the cup. He crawled into my lap. After drinking from the cup, he took my hand again and put the cup back into it. He was no longer crying. I kissed his head and hugged him.

Once, I thought I had lost him. That was when he was first learning to roll around and scoot. I had been doing the dishes and didn't really realize that he'd gotten so good at getting around. I returned to the blanket I had put him on and found that he was gone.

I crawled around on my hands and knees, couldn't find him, and then panicked. I started calling folks. I had lost my son! My heart was pounding, I was sweating, and I wasn't sure whom to call. I couldn't call my social worker, as I was afraid she would deem me unable to care for him, being blind and all. I couldn't call his father, as he didn't have a cell phone, and I didn't know the name of the place where he worked. What to do?

So I started calling my friends from the streets who were in recovery. They knew I was kind of spacey, being both totally blind and a blonde. They might laugh, but they would help me find him. No one answered. No one was home. My goodness, where are people when you need them?

By now a good 45 minutes had passed. I held the phone in one hand while I crawled around on the floor, fearing I would step on him if I stood up, calling and calling for my Ricky.

At last someone answered. I was crying. "I've lost Ricky!" I wailed. "Can you help me find him?"

"What?" I remember her saying.

"He rolled off the blanket, and I can't find him!"

Needless to say, we found him, and he was fine. He had a big grin for my friend when she pulled him from between the couch and chair. I guess he had fallen asleep there. For me, however, it was one of the times I thought my heart was not going to hold out and I was going to have a heart attack, making me really feel my age of 38 with a son less than one year old.

Some people do not have common sense. One time we were eating out at Olive Garden. Someone had given our family a gift card. It was my first visit there, and I loved it. Anyway, I was feeding Ricky, who was in a high chair. He had been paying attention for a bit; he was good about reaching with his mouth to get the food off the spoon if I put the food on it. I suppose he had gotten tired of me missing his mouth. Anyway, I guess he was into the excitement of all the people and the new place. This time, as I put the food up to his face, he must have turned his head, because I heard a lady say loudly, "Ma'am, that's his ear!"

I flushed with embarrassment and told Ricky to turn around. The lady came up to our table and said, "You're blind!" I said, "Well, yes, I am. Did you think I was feeding my son's ear on purpose?"

I remember the first day Ricky showed me that he really understood that I was blind. He had just turned one and was just beginning to walk without holding onto the furniture. I had washed his face and hands after breakfast, and it was time to go out on the porch to wait for the day care bus. Normally I pulled him out of the high chair, stood him up beside it, put the paper towels that I had used to wash his hands in the trash, picked him back up, and took him to the door.

However, this one morning, as I reached down to lift Ricky, he grabbed two of my fingers tightly and started pulling them as he walked. "Where are you taking me?" I asked. Of course he wasn't talking yet, so I just followed along. Sure enough, the little guy walked me directly to the front door and then grabbed at my shirt for me to pick him up. He had just walked me to the door, steering me clear of the doorway that we normally ran into daily as we walked to the door. All I could say, as I felt tears in my eyes, was, "How did you get so smart?"

Once he was talking, of course things got a lot easier. We became a team, helping one another to get through day–to–day tasks. But as he's aged and grown, we've continually faced new challenges. Now that he's in school, the main challenge is the educational process, as I try to help him learn to read and do homework. As he gets involved in activities, I long to see him — literally SEE him — receive school awards or play in a soccer game. But we both know that can never be.

It also makes me sad when he says that he wishes we could go to the park and play. However, I choose not to do that, given that I'm unable to watch him, to protect him. I know from my own life experiences that there are some very cruel people in the world, and I want to protect him from all that as best I can. Likewise, if he were to fall and get hurt, I fear that I wouldn't have the ability to help him.

But somehow, he always understands. I learn so much from him! We figure out together how to assemble things. He looks at the pictures and explains to me what to do. And now that he's learning to read, he can read me directions, too.

Seeing the world from his viewpoint has been such a growing experience for me! I cherish each and every moment with him. And whenever I doubt any of my own abilities, due to my blindness, he's always there to hug me and say, "It's okay, Mom. We'll figure it out!"

Chapter 24

And He Is Only Three

He walks Mommy to the restroom door at a store or at church, places her hand on the women's door, and says, "There you go." And he is only three.

He walks Mommy to a church pew, being careful to make sure no one else is seated there. He places her hand on the seat where she is to sit. And he is only three.

He waits at the bottom of the stairs to take Mommy's hand to walk her to a waiting car. He places her hand on the door handle, saying, "There you go." And he is only three.

He helps Mommy vacuum, saying, "Mommy, you missed some stuff. I'll do it." And he is only three.

He tells Mommy "Not that" when she's searching for green beans and has corn instead. "Let me help you," he says, and gently places the green beans in her hand. Again he says, "There you go." And he is only three.

He asks Mommy to go to the park, and Mommy has to say, "No, I'm sorry, but Mommy can't see, so she can't take you to the park. Mommy couldn't keep you safe if you were to fall or if something else were to happen."

He then takes Mommy's hand and says, "Come, Mommy."

He walks me outside, where he has set two patio chairs side by side, facing the porch. He says, "Sit down and put your feet on the stairs." Then he says, "Roll your window down; it's hot and sunny outside," although it's actually winter and bitter cold.

So I ask, "Where are we going, Ricky?"

He replies, "We're going to the park. I'll drive and will make sure you're safe."

And he is only three.

Chapter 25

Having My Remaining Eye Removed

I knew I had to have my remaining eye removed, and I wondered: Would I then be in total darkness, pitch black? The eye had become so painful! I was living day to day in chronic pain, made tearful from each movement, having held onto my last eye as long as I possibly could. Then, no longer able to sleep due to the pain, for weeks I prayed for the pain to lessen so I could hold onto my eye for just one more day. I was praying for something concrete with stem cell research to come along, something that would allow them a shot at saving my eye. Then maybe I could try again.

However, as my blood pressure was up, and due to the chronic pain, I simply couldn't go on like that much longer, and I knew it. Making the call to have the second eye taken out was such a painful call, though, knowing that once it was gone, both my eyes would be gone for good: both taken out in just three years.

I went totally blind in less than 72 hours. Think about that. Less than 72 hours! If that's not a life-changing event, I don't know what is. But then I had to come to terms with the idea of not just being blind, but with having my eyeballs totally removed as well. It was mind-boggling to me. I mean, you think about teeth being pulled, but *eyes* being taken out? That was something that had never been on my radar. Never in my wildest, drug-induced dreams, with all the horrors I could fathom, had the idea of living in total darkness ever crossed my mind.

My heart ached; I was grieving daily. For so long, I had held out hope for a medical solution to my problem. I had held out hope for any chance at saving my sight, no matter how small that chance might have been. I knew that once both my eyes were gone, I would never see again. I would never have even the chance to see my son. Never again would I be able to see the blue of the sky, which I had taken for granted for so many years.

As I said before, eyeball removal does not constitute a hospital stay. Gosh, you'd think that at least it would merit some kind of grief counseling. But no, not in this day and age. So much now is done on an outpatient basis, and that includes this type of surgery. You're in and out, minus your eyeball, in three hours. That sounds just plumb crazy, doesn't it?

Now I had two eyeballs gone, and what a headache!

When I had my first eyeball removed, my head felt a little lopsided. This time, when I had the second eyeball removed, that same strange, lopsided feeling returned.

And here was something else to ponder. With both my eyes gone, so much for the eyes being the windows to the soul! At least I knew that mine would never be that again.

They told me that in a few weeks, I would get a new prosthetic eye. I wondered if they could match it to the one I already had. I wondered if the new eye would have embroidery thread to make the blood vessels, and if the eye would be hand painted. Well, in a few weeks, I would find out.

I giggled when I set the appointment to get my first prosthetic eye made, as they gave me the name and number of a dentist that made eyeballs.

I laughed, "Are you kidding me?"

But it was no joke. I called to set up the appointment, and it was really and truly a dentist's office.

The guy was very interesting. He told war stories as he

poured a mixture of clay and algae into my open, empty eye socket.

I should probably attempt to explain what it's like to "see" through empty sockets. Is it total darkness? Well, sort of. Number one, it sucks, because with both eyeballs removed, there's zero chance of restoring the sight, as whole eyeball transplants are not doable as of now. It has something to do with the reconnection of the optic nerve. Anyway, what I see now is a thick, unmoving, dark, gloomy kind of off–gray. It seems endless. It's as if you're raising your head to look at an object, but the look is an endless nothingness. It's not a solid blackness, and I have to say that's good, because I'm kind of scared of the dark and the things that lurk in it. Instead, it's a dark, endless gray.

The new prosthetics guy was not a dentist. He explained that he would replace my first prosthesis so he could make a matching set of new prosthetic eyeballs. He was great, very funny.

"Do you have a photo?" he asked.

"Of what?"

"Of you before they took out your eyes."

"No," I said. "The other guy didn't ask for a photo. Is that standard?" No one had told me that a photo would be expected.

"Okay. So what color do you want your new eyes to be?"

"Well, they used to be a sort of gray–blue, turning yellow-green in the sun."

"You'll have to pick a color. These won't be changing ones."

I thought for a minute. Then I asked, "What am I wearing?"

"A black and blue–green dress."

"So does it look good on me?"

He laughed. "Yes, it's a great color for you."

"Fine," I said. "Let's make the eyes match this dress."

"Really?"

"Sure, why not? You said it looks great on me!"

So that's what he did. Getting the right color for prosthetic eyeballs does not have to be a challenge. But if you want the new eyeballs to match the clothes you're wearing that day, it had better be a great color for eyeballs.

***

My heart was often sad after that. With both of my real eyes gone, it was a grieving process for sure. I could also tell that as each day passed, Matt was drawing further and further from me. For him, too, I think the removal of the second eye had meant the loss of hope. I think we both thought that as long as I could keep that second eye, there would still be hope that my sight could be restored, and some sort of normalcy of our past relationship prior to blindness could be restored. But now both the eye and the hope were gone.

At that surgery, unlike all the others, Matt wasn't present. I went home with friends, who took care of me while I recovered. Matt kept Ricky at our home. But deep in my soul, in my heart of hearts, I felt that this would be the straw that broke the camel's back, so to speak, for our relationship. Our shared hope that I would see again one day was now gone, and by now, that was really all we had left in our relationship.

I was a changed person: totally blind, needing help to find a bathroom, always needing to hold onto an arm, needing help with shopping and with so many other things. It was just not the same as it had been when I was sighted and we hung out and fell in love. I was dependent upon Matt for so many of my day-to-day tasks!

However, with each new day, I was moving forward, able to manage with less and less — learning, for example, that it was best if I didn't go to the store with him, as then he had both Ricky and me attached to his arm or the basket. In short, I knew that it was a big adjustment for Matt, and I know he tried, but it wore on him daily.

He had stepped up to take care of me when I could not take care of myself. Somehow, however, I think he resented it all. He did the right thing for the situation we had been dealt, which was taking care of me until I learned to take care of myself. But all of it together — having to place our daughter for adoption, my loss of sight, the removal of both my eyes, and no more hope for vision for me after that — was life–changing for both of us.

And indeed, that was the tipping point for our relationship. Soon, Matt moved out, and I struggled when he left.

A lesson I can take from all this is that a life–changing event will either make you or break you, and ours broke us. However, I am and always will be thankful to Matt for seeing me through those awful times and for being a constant father in his son's life, both then and now.

Chapter 26

My First Mainstream Job

There I was at last, seeking work as a newly blind person with a long criminal history. As they say sarcastically nowadays, "Good luck with that!" But I had to try.

I visited the unemployment office, asking for assistance. As a sighted person, I had had only one meager job; that was at McDonald's for about six months. Now, with my very noticeable disability, the odds were most certainly against my getting hired. I had three major things working against me: society's preconceived notions of how much (or how little) a blind person can do, my criminal background, and my almost total lack of a work history.

For my first visit to the unemployment office, I used Paratransit. This is a public system created to run with regular bus systems, but providing door-to-door service for those of us without sight, with limited mobility, or with other barriers that might leave us struggling to ride a regular public bus.

My driver walked me through the door and up to the counter, and then left. The bus would return in five hours to pick me up. I wanted to allow plenty of time, as I had no idea how long it would take to register and then get help in seeking employment suitable for a blind ex–offender.

At the counter, I asked to sign up for job seekers' assistance and gave my name. They asked me to take a seat. "Sure," I said, "but where are the seats?" The people at the desk fell silent. "I'm blind," I said. "If you could just tell me what direction the seats are in, that would be great."

A lady walked around and assisted me to the waiting area. That turned out to be just a few steps from the front desk or counter. As I sat there, I listened to the people come and go. They came in, got their names called, stayed for a while, and then left. The day wore on. I had arrived promptly at 9:00 a.m., as they had requested on the phone. So why wasn't my name being called?

I could tell there were lots of people all around. It was indeed a busy place. But why were they too busy to help me? It was now about 12:00 noon. I was aware that there were many people who had arrived after me, but they were leaving before me.

At last I spoke up, saying, "Excuse me, is anyone there at the front counter?" No one responded, yet I could hear them shuffling around. A little louder this time, I said, "Excuse me. I'm blind. I can't see you, but you can see me! I'm here to seek work. Will someone be able to assist me?"

As this was my first time putting myself out there to seek work, I was already feeling inferior, but I knew I had to find work. I had completed my rehab and had also adjusted as well as I could to being blind. So those were two huge obstacles that I had already overcome. I simply had to find a way to do this!

At last someone called my name, and we went to his office. He filled out papers on my behalf, then said, "I'm sorry, but I don't think we can really assist you here." Then he said, "Shouldn't you look into one of those workshop places?"

"What, for $150 a week? Sir, I have a child who needs me. I have to have a job!" I realized I was not going to get any help there, but I still said, "I'll call every week to see if you find something or have any ideas." There was nothing more I could do that day.

I was advocating for myself as best I knew how, but I did

not land a job through that particular agency. I feel sure that I was judged by both my criminal history and my blindness.

Once you're an ex-offender, a felon who has been released, it's very hard to find work. In fact, at least in Missouri, employers don't have to hire any ex-offenders. There is no discrimination protection for ex-offenders. Companies are even allowed to have policies against hiring them.

Most ex-offenders, if they are considered for employment (and that's a very big if), can only get entry-level jobs, such as working in a warehouse, doing yard work, washing dishes, working in fast-food places, or maybe waiting tables at some inexpensive restaurant. But obviously, as a totally blind person, I could not perform any of those jobs. However, I surely could not work at a sheltered workshop all my life, doing piece work, making roughly $150 a week before taxes. An additional problem for me was that I was not eligible for food stamps, due to my felony drug convictions.

As an ex-offender, you soon find that no one — or so it can seem — wants to trust you or help you succeed: not employers, not landlords, not the government, and not even the new friends you try to make.

But I so wanted a better life for my son than living in the projects or state-subsidized apartment dwellings! Isn't that what all parents want for their children? In my heart of hearts, I knew that if I could just find a job, just move us to an area where the school districts have high educational scores, that as my child grew, he would have a better chance. I'm not saying that good kids don't come from the projects, too, but given that I was blind, I had to consider my abilities to protect us and look out for my son.

So I reached out to agencies that help find jobs for those with "non-traditional work histories." Now doesn't that sound better than talking about a person with a criminal history, an ex-offender, or a person with no work history? I think it does for sure!

However, within a few weeks, I realized that they weren't cut out to assist a person with a disability. They could work with my criminal history, also with my limited work history and lack of experience, but they couldn't handle all that plus my blindness. So, once again, I changed my approach, this time reaching out to agencies that place persons with disabilities. But these groups, in turn, seemed puzzled by how to approach the problem of my criminal history. So what was I to do? Where in the working world was I going to fit in? Who was going to give me the chance to even *try* to fit in?

I realize now that all this was part of my attempt to find my path in life. I had already met — and continue to meet — numerous barriers. I often trip on that path. I stumble and sometimes fall, tripped up by the numerous cracks in the system. No, it's not just the system. I will say that society as a whole has some mighty serious cracks in it.

I was in college by now. I had stopped working at the workshop to focus on school. But I could not live as a student with a child and no state resources. As I mentioned above, drug offenders can't *ever* receive food stamps in Missouri, no matter how long they've been clean and off drugs and no matter what their life circumstances might be, such as contracting a chronic illness, or losing their job, or having children, or various other things that can change one's economic status.

Never in one's whole life is a long time. Life does happen, and people do change, but for this there is no gray area, at least not in Missouri. Sex offenders or pedophiles or murderers can walk out of prison and get food stamps if they need them, but those of us with the disease of addiction, a disease that can be arrested and that one can recover from and find a meaningful way of life, as I have done, are judged for our past mistakes for the remainder of our lives.

I knew I had made mistakes. I knew I had to work very

hard, as hard as I had worked at messing up, to earn my way back into the mainstream without judgment. I was more than willing to do that. I just needed someone to give me an opportunity.

It may seem funny, given the past life I had led, that I was simply trying to be a taxpaying member of my community, to earn my way, to provide for my family. Yet it seemed that every agency or case worker I spoke with would always refer me back to a workshop environment. For me, though, that was not an option. My attitude was not due merely to the very limited pay provided by such workshops. After all, I had survived for almost 20 years on the streets. I knew I was smart. I knew, deep down, that I could do more than that type of work, much more.

Thus I continued to develop my advocacy skills, realizing that society was almost surely not going to believe in me. I kept hearing, "Sorry, but I can't help." And for a while, I accepted that. Then I would move on, to hunt up the next resource, the next contact. Whenever I would get another no, I would say, " Okay, then. Any thoughts on whom I might try to contact to help me?" Thus I was building my networking abilities right along with my advocacy skills.

At last a dear friend, Malcolm Garcia, a reporter who had written a series of newspaper stories about me, called me up. He told me about a very large hiring event just for ex–offenders. We thought that my being an active college student might help. Malcolm offered to take me there, act as my advocate, and help me in any way he could.

After waiting in a very long line, we realized that we weren't going to get in to actually speak with anyone. But we did manage to pick up some fliers inside, fliers that listed some resources. Then we began making contact with them.

I finally found a man who had started a service to help ex-offenders find work. He was operating it out of his car, trying to get it off the ground. When I contacted this person, I said, "If you'll give me a chance, I'll work for free for a while. I can contact employers and find out if they'll hire felons, and if so, which felons they'll consider, felons with what kinds of charges. Then you'll have a pool of 'felon friendly' employers, so you can open doors for your clients as you get them."

I wasn't eager to work for free, but I saw this as a first step, a necessary one. In effect, I had to sell myself, sell my personality and my enthusiasm, before I could expect to get paid for my work. I was in school, true, but this job would give me a needed work history. I could even do the job from home, making cold calls to employers in our city.

At least it was a start. This would be real work, something I could put on an application, and it was something I could do as a blind person. At the same time, I would be getting lots of contacts. Maybe I would run across a felon–friendly place that would have jobs that I myself could be considered for.

As the man's operation grew, I began getting paid $100 a week. True, it was even less than what the workshop paid, but it was a mainstream job.

So I continued, all the while developing my networking abilities and my computer skills, and I started working with the ex–offenders who were seeking work. At last, the man I was working for (an ex–offender himself) no longer had to work from his car. He got an office, and he was starting to receive funding. I started doing phone screenings from home, screening ex–offenders, finding out what their crimes were, what kind of work they had done or could do. Then I would connect them with the list of places I had contacted.

I only worked there for six months total and never went to the office. I was also a board member for this fledgling, growing, not–for–profit organization. It was not too shabby for my first job, even if it had taken a lot of effort to get it. At last I knew I had built some real skills. They always say that it's best to be working while you're looking for a new job, and I was doing both.

By this time, we had moved. After the stem cell project fell through, a few donors chose to allow us to keep the funds for my adaptive needs. This allowed us to purchase a tiny trailer house (the one I mentioned at the end of Chapter 20) on a hill just a few blocks from the Raytown city limits and within a few blocks of Independence, Missouri. Those are both suburbs of the much larger Kansas City, Missouri. We no longer lived in the 'hood. True, we lived in an old, rundown trailer park, but for me, this meant that we were one step closer to the suburbs. The trailer was 20 years old and needed a whole lot of work, but what can you expect for $4,000? To its advantage, it had a fenced yard and a place for a washer and dryer.

Just days after we had moved in, I was doing dishes one day and using my adaptive technology, screen–reading software program. This converts text information on the computer to speech. I was reading the help wanted ads on Craigslist. I was still in college, but it was summer, and I was only taking one course at the time. I carefully reviewed the job information. A listing that really caught my attention was for one at a new office opening in Kansas City. It was a job helping people with sight impairments find work. Now how perfectly perfect was that? And it paid $8.00 an hour!

Who could be better at this job than I would be? Who better to find a job for a blind person than another blind person? And I was currently doing job development for a non–profit. I already had all those contacts that would hire felons. Surely I could contact them to find out their views of the sight impaired. So it seemed to me that I would be a perfect match.

I was so excited, and I called to set up an interview. My line was, "Hey, I'm helping ex–felons find work. Surely I can help the blind!" They set up an interview for me. I mailed them my résumé, but did not tell them that I was totally without sight.

I was given an address. Now, I had lived on the streets for

years, and I knew most of the streets in Kansas City. Realizing I had no idea where this was, I called back. We all laughed. They had given me their address in Springfield, Missouri, as they had not yet rented an office space in Kansas City. So I said I'd wait and meet the person to head the office in Kansas City and interview then. Again, I did not share that I was blind.

I remember the man who called me for an interview. He told me that his boss really liked me from just speaking to me on the phone. He gave me the day he would be in the KC office and set up the interview. I had classes that day and it was my gym day. I called the man back and said, "You know, I have gym class right before the interview appointment. Will you be offended if I arrive in workout clothes?" Because I had to use public transportation, I knew there was no way I could shower, change, and make it to the interview in time.

He said that would be fine. I assured him that if there was a second interview, I would dress properly. He laughed.

When that day came, I arrived at an office building in downtown Kansas City. There were businesspeople everywhere. There was a coffee shop in the building, even a restaurant. I knew from my sighted life where I was. I knew where these high-rise buildings were. As I waited for my interview, I couldn't help but reflect. Wow! A job in an office building, after all the things I had been through? And $8.00 an hour? That was equally amazing to me.

We interviewed at last. I said, "If I can help criminals, I'm sure I can handle job placement for the vision impaired."

"I'm sorry," he said, "because I really like you. But you're blind, and I need someone to drive clients. I just don't see how this could work." I reminded him that I was placing ex-offenders from my home, without ever going anywhere. Again, he said no.

He escorted me downstairs, where I had to wait for my bus.

"How did you get here?" he asked.

"Public transportation," I answered.

"Well, it was great to meet you," he said, and left.

A few minutes later, he was back, saying, "Do you want to take a look at our office?" I was puzzled, but I said, "Sure!" Yeah, the blind girl will love to see the office. He had only hired one person so far, so it was just those two at the time.

I met her. As we rode down in the elevator, he said, "I'm sorry. I sure wish I could have hired you." I went back to my seat in the lobby. But as I continued to wait for my ride, he returned once again. He said he had spoken with his boss, and they had all agreed we would at least give it a try. If it didn't work, it didn't work. I would start the following week.

My eyes filled with tears. My ride arrived and I returned home, pinching myself.

The office was new and growing, so we had a handful of clients. We worked three days a week, six hours a day. I was really earning a paycheck! I felt hope. I had tremendous gratitude. After all those years of being on the streets, after all that I had struggled with since becoming blind, I felt for the first time that I was a whole person.

Given my past, it was hard to believe. There I was, gainfully employed and helping others, working for a little non-profit. People trusted me, and I was darned good at what I did. What a far cry from being a street corner prostitute, stealing food from a 7-11 store, and relieving myself outside like a animal. Now I had an office downtown. How cool was that?

I loved my job. I was not only doing job development, but I was answering phones and getting client referrals. Before I knew it, I had a full case load of my own. There was even coffee being delivered every morning to my desk in our little office in that fancy office building in downtown KC.

Daily, I was in awe. How far I had come! God had opened this door. Now I just had to keep doing the next right thing. The more right I did, the more doors opened.

We were off and running. We started having employers

calling the office, asking for people. Our office took on many shapes, and we opened new offices. I simply loved coming up with ways for sight–impaired people to find jobs. Many of our clients had been in sheltered workshops, so there, too, I had walked in their shoes.

Basically, I just loved helping people. Maybe that came from so many years of people not helping me, so I wanted to be the one to say yes. I wanted to be the one to believe in our clients and their abilities. The job also provided a way to help my friends who were drug–free and off the streets. I was able to give them the chance to do more with their lives.

I started out as a job developer, and then I was named Program Assistant. Wow again. A title! Eventually, I became the Program Supervisor. I dropped out of college, as my life was full.

Now I was getting $10 an hour and working four days a week, as our office was closed on Fridays. I was still doing my little street outreach Brown Bag Fridays, as well, and soon my boss joined in.

Chapter 27

The House Next Door to Mary Christine

However, in contrast to my working life, my personal life was a real roller coaster.

As I said before, after I had my remaining eye taken out, Matt chose to end our relationship. When he informed me at last that he was moving out of town, he had already moved out of our home. He had been seeing someone and was moving in with her in the St. Charles/St. Louis area.

For a while, he would drive the four hours between St. Louis and Kansas City to get Ricky and then drive him back. But then Ricky turned five, and Matt and I both knew there was no way this was going to work once Ricky started school.

Matt was still active in his son's life, taking Ricky a few days a week and on weekends. But Matt and I were over, and both my eyes had been removed. If it hadn't been for my wonderful job, I would have been in despair. It was only that job — plus the responsibility of being Ricky's mom, of course — that kept me going. It was often hard to smile, though.

There was one other bright spot in my life. Mary Christine's adoptive parents and I had stayed in touch via e-mail, phone calls, and visits when we were able.

I was thrilled by one particular e-mail from them. The house next door to them was for sale. They thought it would be terrific if Ricky and I could move in next to them. They could help me with Ricky's educational process, and Ricky and Mary

Christine could grow up together as brother and sister. *How insane*, some might think. But Mary Christine is lucky. She has two moms that love her.

Given that they lived across the state from us, in St. Louis, and in a super-nice community, not the 'hood, like us, I knew there was no way I could afford this. I had a great job — at least it was great for me — but I was only making $12 an hour. That seemed like riches to me, but in reality, I had no credit to buy a house with, not with all my years on the streets. And at the time, I had a total of only three years of employment beyond the six-month stint at McDonald's before my blindness.

Thrilled by the concept of this plan, but knowing it was not something I could do by myself, we decided to see if we could find supporters. We found someone willing to pledge funds and another person to pledge work on the place. And believe me, the place needed lots of work! So we chose to see if we could get some community support via the media.

We placed a bid on the house after visiting it and showing it to Mary Christine and Ricky. They ran through the empty house, laughing like long–lost friends reunited. It was almost as if they had never been separated.

The countdown was on. I spent most of my free time calling around, looking for ways to get things to fix the house or to find people to help us make this dream come true. I so wanted to live next door to the daughter I had put up for adoption. How wonderful it would be if Ricky and she could be part of each other's lives! Having the biological mom and the adoptive mom living next door to each other, sharing a yard — now that is not your typical family dynamic for sure! But we both felt it would be great for us and our families.

A few news stories were filmed, and one newspaper story was run. However, most of the pieces were not going to be shown or run until we closed on the house. We believed that once we closed on the house and all the stories came out, we would get the funds needed to cover this house — a real house, in a little community with a good school and opportunities for Ricky that I knew I couldn't provide where we were in Kansas City.

With Matt having left, and with both my eyes gone for good, I really needed this positive thing in my life. This was a new spring of hope, a new chance to move forward, and I was very excited by the prospect. There were many e-mails between Mary Christine's adoptive mom and me as we both worked hard to raise the necessary funds.

It was really hard to juggle everything, though. There I was, trying to work full time and having to use public transportation, so my days were long. Sometimes in the mornings, I would have to leave at 5:30 in order to get to work by 8:00. I would leave work at 4:00, and often not get home until 7:00. The Paratransit I used had a large window for pick-ups, and of course their buses did not run as frequently as the regular city buses. In the winter months, they would often run late. You might have to share a ride with up to five other people, and they might all get dropped off before you made your destination, so your ride could be very long and tiring.

I would come home, cook, and spend as much time as I could with Ricky. Sometimes I think that able-bodied people and those with sight take for granted being able to drive to the store, find what they need, walk back to their car, and drive home. But that is not the life of your typical person with a disability.

Sometimes I would be picked up by my ride at 6:00 a.m., be the only rider that morning, and be dropped off at work really quickly. Then I would have to stand outside for over an hour until the building opened at 7:30. The next day, I might get picked up at 5:30 and not get to the office until 8:00. But if I wanted to work a real job, be part of the mainstream, and take care of myself and my child, then this was what I had to do. I would run ads looking for people in car pools, and sometimes that worked out. But I never found a steady car pool driver, so Paratransit for the disabled was my main form of travel. It often felt like a job in itself.

But back to the house.

We grew more and more excited as the days passed, each one bringing us one day closer to the closing date. Every day, it seemed, we made new plans, envisioning what it would be like to live in a real house that would someday be ours.

During this time, we had an overnight visit with Mary Christine's adoptive parents. Once again, we explored the house we so hoped to get, with Ricky and Mary Christine running through the echoing hallways of the old house, laughing together. At the sleepover in Mary Christine's bedroom, however, a miracle happened to me after we had all lain down to sleep. I was awakened by Mary Christine, and she asked to get in bed with me. I paused, as I was very surprised by the request, but of course I said yes and made room. As she snuggled in the bed beside me, I touched her soft hair, listening to her every breath, taken back to the months she was in my tummy and I was praying for her life, praying that she would make it into the world. Before the night was over, Ricky had climbed into bed with me, too, so I had both my little ones, one on each side, snuggled up with me. it was a moment in time I'll never forget.

Sadly, though, the dream house was not to be ours. Here's what happened.

Mary Christine's adoptive parents had a number of other adopted children, and they started to rethink the whole thing. The thought of perhaps not being able to raise enough funds after we closed on the house, then having to find some other way to pay for it, was causing them fear. The night before the bid we had submitted was to be lowered, we learned that someone had placed a higher bid. Just hours before we were going to close on the house and all the news stories were going to run, we learned that with our lowered bid, we would not get the house.

Once again, I was heartbroken. Ricky and I were both sad. He had been so excited, and I had tried so hard! I had had so much faith that if I had been saved from the life I had lived on the streets, then surely this wonderful thing would happen, too. After the long fight to save my sight, to save my eyeballs, I had believed in my heart of hearts that this dream would come true, when so many others had failed.

So there I was again, struggling just to get out of bed to face each day, trying to explain to Ricky why he was not going to live next door to his sister. Indeed, it was hard for all of us.

Chapter 28

Our Move, Then Another Disappointment

I struggled to make the best decisions, the right ones. In Kansas City, I was working on a macro-level with an agency in my free time. I was still helping the disabled from my downtown office, but I had expanded ways to give back. One way was by working to get a bill passed, one that would allow drug offenders in Missouri to be considered for food stamps if their economic status changed for the worse due to any number of reasons. If the person had been drug free and was willing to take a urine test to show they were drug free, then they too, just like all other Americans, could be considered for this economic assistance, this temporary hand up during tough times, if needed.

I was also able to encourage employers to hire ex-offenders by pointing out to them that this would help create safer communities. It has been proven that if ex-offenders can find jobs, they are less apt to re-offend.

I had dug in my heels. I was active in many areas of my Kansas City community, making yearly trips to the capital, Jefferson City, to lobby and testify. I had also taken on a role in the community with my son's daycare.

I was also involved with a very special program of urban bus tours called "The City You Never See." The goal of these tours is to educate the community about inner-city poverty. This project has been in the news quite often, and it's now starting in other cities, as well. For these tours, we would load up community leaders, politicians, judges, medical professionals, social workers, and others for a bus ride through town, stopping in our community's worst streets. At each stop, a person would step onto the bus and share their story about that community. I would step on and tell about the park I had lived in for nearly two decades — also telling how, now that I no longer lived in the park, I took food and coats there for others.

I was so connected to my community there in Kansas City! I was finding opportunities to share my story, to help change people. I was giving hugs of hope to my street friends, and by day I was working to help the disabled find gainful employment. I was truly torn at the thought of leaving all this behind, but I wanted and needed for Ricky to be closer to both his father and his sister, and I knew that once Ricky started school, I would need his father's support.

I first tried to have my little trailer moved. However, it was in pretty bad shape and was deemed unmovable. So I sold it for two grand, and stepped out in faith.

I found us a little one–bedroom apartment in the suburbs, just a couple of minutes from where Ricky's father had started his new life in St. Charles/St. Louis. It was very sad that we had not been able to get the house next door to Mary Christine, but I knew I would be a mere 30 minutes away from her, and Ricky would no longer have to ride four hours to visit his father.

I still mourn the things and friends I left behind. But Ricky is in a wonderful school, and the company I was working for in Kansas City had an office in the St. Louis area, so I was able to transfer there.

For me, as a blind person, adjustment to a new community has not been easy. All of our friends and the entire support system I had built are in Kansas City. Often, even after being here in St. Louis for a year, I feel isolated.

When we first moved to our little apartment last year, I was attempting to put Ricky's things together. I remember sitting on the floor, crying that I just couldn't do it. I wanted to, but I couldn't figure it all out. He hugged me and said, "Mom, it's okay!" Then he said something that still gives me chills when I think about it. He said, "When we're in Heaven, we'll be able to run and play and you won't be blind anymore!" Needless to say, I cried even more then.

Recently, though, another major blow fell. My great job, the one I loved so much, is over. The company I had worked for from 2008, Community Employment, shut all its offices statewide. I have been struggling to find work ever since.

The bill for food stamps for drug felons never passed, so I'm still unable to tap into that. I've had a number of interviews and have submitted many applications, but I'm finding myself back at square one. The folks that help ex–offenders don't know what to do with the blind part, and the blind folks and people who work with the disabled are unsure what to do with the ex–offender part!

I often question, thinking, Gosh, maybe my dreams are too big — both a job and a house! What right do I have to imagine that I might get all that? After all, many of the friends I was on the streets with are dead.

But God — or something — has kept me alive and has brought me this far. I know there is a purpose to all this, and even without an explanation, I do believe. I believe that if I keep trying, keep doing the next right thing, keep fighting to live on the right side, keep being a good mom and righting wrongs, I believe — I *know* — that we will be blessed. How exactly that blessing will look or feel, I don't know. But I do believe. I did not survive all those years without some purpose, and that I know without a doubt.

So I will continue seeking work. I have faith, and I know that God will open a door.

Meanwhile, all this has given me time to write my story

down in a book!

Chapter 29

Our Open Adoption: Redefining Adoption

It seemed fitting, somehow, to give this subject its own chapter.

By now you've read about many of my — our — ups and downs. You can see that I've made many, many choices during my life. In the past, I made choices as an addict. Now, I make choices as a mom. Making choices, making decisions, becomes easier with each passing day, but of course many decisions are still very hard to make.

I remember that days after I had arrived to live with Matt, and weeks after the birth of our little girl, Mary Christine, we received a life–changing letter. At that time, Mary Christine was still in the hospital, with a long road of surgeries and other challenges ahead of her. We were still grieving the loss of our little girl to adoption, but also the loss of my sight and all the changes that had brought to our life and our relationship.

The letter was from Mary Christine's adoptive mom.

At first, after I left the hospital where Mary Christine was born and I was released back to the prison hospital to continue my recovery, I would get calls from the doctors who were caring for Mary Christine. They would explain what was going on: what operations she would have, as they would come in phases, and then the outcome of each operation. This had been arranged by Mary Christine's adoptive mom, to allow me to at least know what was going on. This was not something that she had to do for me, but she wanted to, because I had told her that I had planned to care for our little girl, but could not. That is, Mary Christine's adoptive mom knew that I loved my child and had not simply abandoned her.

At first, with every passing moment, I feared that Mary Christine wouldn't make it, so being allowed calls from the hospital to be kept informed brought me a lot of comfort. However, as each day passed, it became clearer that she was more and more out of danger of death. It was wonderful of the prison hospital to allow me to take these calls. Given that I had placed Mary Christine for adoption, they were under no obligation to allow them. I felt truly blessed by having these people in control of my life. They saw the situation and acted as more than just guards; they acted as human beings.

Matt opened the very long letter from Mary Christine's adoptive parents and read it to me. We both cried, because they were opening a door for us. They said they understood our situation, but when we were ready, we could have a relationship with them and our daughter on whatever level we felt comfortable with.

I had spoken to the adoptive mom on the phone before. She had called me after the nice lawyer had passed my information on to her and she had researched the medical conditions our little girl would be facing, as well as the many outcomes that might be in store. After that, I had met her in person. I was in shackles in the county courthouse, still in prison custody, taking medication every hour on the hour to keep my eyeballs from rupturing from movement. We spoke, and at that time, they gave me a card offering continued contact. But that was just days after the birth, and I was simply not ready, then, as it was too painful. Now weeks had passed, and I felt ready for this at last.

When Matt and I received that long letter, I hadn't spoken to the adoptive parents since the last time at the courthouse.

That was when I had terminated my rights to my daughter, thus allowing her to be raised by other parents, a couple who could provide far better medical care than Matt and I could, thereby giving our daughter her best fighting chance at life.

Who would ever have guessed that our phone call on Father's Day, just six weeks after Mary Christine's birth, would spark visits, play dates, sleepovers, phone calls and e-mails throughout her little life? And once Ricky arrived, we agreed to keep those two siblings, who were a mere 10 months apart, in each other's lives.

Mary Christine knows that I grew her in my tummy. Ricky knows that she shares me and his father, Matt, as parents. Each time the two are together, they are like longtime friends. It's as though they had never spent a day apart.

I believe that this relationship is healing for me. And for Ricky and Mary Christine, it will pave the way for a lifelong relationship between them. They will not have to grow up with any questions about who their parents or siblings are. They have truly bonded.

We love our sleepovers at Mary Christine's house, as those allow me, as well, to have a relationship with my daughter, whom I have always loved so very much. All the other children in the home welcome Ricky with each visit, so it's truly as if we're an extension of their family.

Sometimes I'm sad after our visits, missing Mary Christine and her life. But as I said before, where we live now, in St. Louis, we're just 30 minutes from their home, so we get to visit far more often than we could when Ricky and I still lived in Kansas City. Ricky is always quick to show off the photos on our walls when visitors come. When they ask, "Who's the little girl in the photos?" he jumps to say, "That's my sister!"

Reading stories of adoptions, I see that most are closed. But I wouldn't change a thing about our unusual arrangement. Along with Mary Christine's adoptive parents, I believe that it's the right thing for the kids.

I love my relationship with Mary Christine's adoptive mom, and I savor every visit with our daughter. I consider Mary Christine's adoptive mom to be my friend. That friendship, just like any other, has its ups and downs. However, we always seem to keep grounded, to stay focused on the main point of our relationship. That's the relationship between our children, the two siblings. Our relationship to one another, as the two moms, is just an added bonus!

We had dreamed of raising the children next door to one another, but that didn't work out. As always, I'm sure that something greater than I am simply had a different plan, so Ricky and I continue on with our visits and overnight stays as often as possible, nurturing the relationship as much as we can.

I'm often touched when Mary Christine's adoptive mom sees something of me in Mary Christine. I always chuckle, and we wonder whether it's a case of nature or nurture. Mary Christine is not around me daily, yet both she and Ricky have many of my characteristics, and they share personality traits. So, during almost every visit, there is at least some discussion of where such traits might have come from.

I think that sharing a child whom one has adopted takes a mighty big heart, but including Mary Christine, her adoptive parents have seven adopted miracles and one birth child of their own, so that speaks volumes about their open hearts.

Now I know that if our Mary Christine has questions as she gets older, that I, her adoptive parents, and Ricky, her biological sibling, will all be here to answer them. She'll never have to go searching. I think that helps build a child with self–esteem, one with secure knowledge of where he or she comes from. That's something that has to remain unresolved for many, many adoptive children.

I'm quite sure that it was not a mistake to build a relationship with Mary Christine or her adoptive parents, and I know they agree. Our frequent sleepovers and e-mails are proof of that.

Thus I encourage other birth moms and adoptive moms to opt for open adoption. As we've seen, it can lead to a beautiful relationship that allows healing for the birth mom — and, later on, for the adopted child.

Chapter 30

Brain Port Study

If someone who had had both eyes taken out was given a chance to be in a test study for a device that could greatly enhance their quality of life, you would think that would be a no-brainer. However, I was sitting there in tears, struggling, trying to figure out what to do.

I had been asked to come in for a screening regarding being a candidate to test a device that works inside the mouth. With electrical pulses on the tongue, it draws the shapes of objects around you, so even people totally without sight, like me, can gather information about their surroundings. For this study, they were seeking a number of people who were blind or nearly blind, so they could see how functional the device was in day-to-day life.

However, I was unsure even whether to call to confirm the appointment for the screening.

Crazy, huh, after all my previous attempts to get just a glimmer of sight, just enough to see my children for the first time. However, this would not be like sight. Just as a cane takes in information about the ground and obstacles in front of you, this device would allow me to understand the objects around me without sight, but with the use of electrical pulses on the tongue.

When I submitted my application, I guess I didn't really think they would take me. By this time, I had learned to live blind, and this device, although it could be quite helpful, would not allow me to see my children's faces or the blue of the sky.

But faced with the necessity of calling to set up the meeting, I found myself in total fear. It was fear of a number of things. What if this device really could allow me to navigate my surroundings without needing assistance from another person — or clumsily, with my white cane? What if, with the newfound tool, I was tempted to use drugs again? I pondered that huge question. Could it be that my blindness was the only thing that had kept me off drugs all that time?

But there was such a passion in my heart, such a strong desire for anything that could help me! How could I say no to this? What if it would allow me to do more with Ricky, given that he always wishes and prays for sight for me? To take part in this project, I would have to go away for a while, for almost a full month, to learn to use the device. Then I would be allowed to bring it home and attempt to use it in everyday life, making detailed records for another 11 months of how it enhanced my daily activities.

I remember speaking to Ricky about my going away, telling him why. He was so excited for me. He listed for me all the things we could do together, telling me we could order pizza and he would show me all the things in the house. Obviously, he was totally not understanding that the device would not allow me to *see* the way he does. He was so excited, and I had fought for so long to see, and there had been so many failed attempts. What if I went and this device simply did not enhance my quality of life? What if it turned out to be another disappointment?

It was a very strange mixture of emotions. I had had a pretty steady life for a while, with no big roller coaster bumps to mess with my emotions. I found that my largest fear, actually, was that the device might work. That's because there was no way I could really know how such a big change in my life might affect me emotionally.

I had listened to the videos about the people who had tested the device in its early stages somewhere. They were able to learn the feeling of letters on their tongue and play cards; some could walk through doorways without assistance. And all of this was merely from electrical pulses on the tongue. It was an exciting prospect, for sure. A lot of training would be required to understand the information my tongue and brain would be receiving, but it seemed to work pretty well for those people on the videos.

Every day, Ricky would return home from school and ask me, "Did you call yet?" And I would have to answer, "No." He had so much hope; how could I let the little guy down by not even trying? So I contacted Ricky's father and asked if he would be willing and able to keep Ricky if I were to go away for a few weeks. Matt's answer was, "Sure!"

So at last I made the call.

It was funny. Once I made the call to set up the appointment, I myself started to feel excitement.

The appointment was to be in just a couple of weeks, so I didn't have much time to get ready to be gone for a month. I had to figure out a place to stay, so I reached out to church friends, to see if they knew any folks in the area where the closest study was being held, about 600 miles from my home. We found a family willing to host me for this study. They would get me to and from the facility for my daily training throughout the entire time that I would need to be out of state and away from Ricky.

I have to be honest. As I'm now blind, going to new places alone, being in unfamiliar surroundings, is very frightening to me. When we go places, Ricky acts as my eyes. He tells me about our surroundings, guides me around, and helps me buy things at the store. This trip, however, I would be taking all alone, with no friends and no Ricky to accompany me.

The day of my journey, when I was trying to get to my bus, was really wild and crazy. My mind was racing. I was terrified that I would miss the bus. We stopped on the way there and asked five different people for directions, and we were given five different sets of directions to the bus station and then to the right line inside the station. Good grief, could it really be that difficult?

At last we found the right line, and what a line it was!

"How many people are there in front of me?" I asked.

"Fifteen," a man answered.

"Yikes!" I said. "How much time do we have before the bus leaves?"

"Just under an hour."

So we waited. And waited. I had never realized before then just how long the lines in a bus station can be, or what all the smells are like. With each passing person, it seemed, I encountered a new smell: wine, beer, cigarettes, body odor, food. It seemed that each person who passed had his or her own smell. Some smells were pleasant, but most of them were not.

At long last, I was in line to board the bus. I was given a control number that would let folks know I had a disability. However, the conversations I had overheard during the hour-long wait to be allowed to get near the loading dock had convinced me that there were many people there who had much worse disabilities than my blindness.

At last I was on the bus and seated. *Okay*, I thought, *here we go.* I was off on my journey, perhaps to a much better life. Was it really possible that a device I would wear on my tongue would allow me to navigate my surroundings without sighted assistance?

The bus driver lightened things up for us. He had a lot of personality, making jokes in a southern drawl. With his clear, deep voice and his wit, he would have made a great radio host.

***

I arrived. Stepping off the bus, I was greeted by one of the people who would be assisting me in getting to and from my appointments. I was to eat and then go straight to the facility to get started.

A little later, I was sitting in the lobby. "Christine?" a woman asked.

"Yes," I answered.

She offered her arm and guided me to an office.

"I'll be working with you for the next few weeks," she said. "But first, we have some tests and paperwork to complete."

"Sure," I said.

We sat down, and she began reading lots of papers and information about the days to come, also about the research itself. At last, I was able to sign and move forward. They also called in a witness, someone who could testify that I understood everything we had talked about.

First, there was a mental exam, to ensure that I was mentally stable. Passed. The next test had to do with depression. Passed.

"So far, so good," the lady said.

Then there was object recognition. "We have to make sure that you know what certain shapes are and such," she said.

"Okay," I said, "but I have no eyeballs. How am I supposed to recognize an object I can't touch?"

"Just guess," she said.

"Seriously?" I asked. But yes, she was serious.

She placed 21 different objects on the table in 21 separate steps. I just had to guess what was there in front of me each time. This was the next test in the lineup.

"You failed," she said, "but we needed to confirm what your visual abilities are."

I said, "I have no eyeballs. Isn't there a box or something to check for that? Why didn't we just skip this test?"

"No," she said, "there is no such box to check. So we'll just go on."

Emotionally stable. Check.

"Now," she said, "there will be a test in which you'll have to reach for objects."

"Reach for objects? Really?"

"Yes," said the tester. So she set objects on a table in front of me, and I was to reach for the requested object. There were 21 of these as, well.

"Really?" I asked again. "Do we really have to do this?"

She said, "You get one try with each request. Just reach. You'll either get it or not."

Feeling a little strange about this after having just done another vision evaluation, I agreed.

Failed.

"Great," I said. "Now what?"

"We have to make sure you can't see," she said.

So I said again, "Funny. I have no eyeballs, and I have to take yet another exam to prove that I can't see?" I was starting to feel rather peeved, as well as wanting to move on with this whole thing.

The next step was that she would type words on a computer screen with different fonts and degrees of contrast. There would be 21 words. That seemed to be their favorite number. Once again, she said there was no box for her to check that would simply indicate that I couldn't see at all.

"Really?" I asked again. By this time, I was pretty sure that any of my own next words would be words of annoyance. What wasn't helping at all was that by this time, I had gone for over 30 hours with no sleep.

"You failed completely again," she said after the pointless word test.

"Great," I said. "I think!"

Next was a dental exam, so it was off to an office where I would have my tongue photographed. They took a couple of photos of my tongue and then poked it with sharp objects in many different places to see if I could feel the objects or differences in the sensations.

"Okay, all good," the man said.

We walked back to the testing room, where I would be told whether I could continue in the project. We had just a few minutes of our five–hour visit left. The woman asked me if I would like to touch the device and explore it at last.

Excited, I said I would, so she moved a box in front of me. I unzipped it and touched something inside. She walked me through the unpacking of the device. There were cords everywhere, and glasses: from Oakley, yet. "Wow!" I said. "At last I get a pair of Oakleys!"

There was a large object in the center.

"What's that?" I asked

"That the camera," she said.

We continued unpacking the device. She had me plug a cord into a small box. After I had done that, she handed me a corded object with a plastic case at the end of it.

"What's this?" I asked.

"This is the mouthpiece," she said.

"Wow, okay."

It was much larger than I had thought it would be, which was about the size of a postage stamp. At least that was what I had read in the paperwork that had been e–mailed to me. This thing was far larger than any stamp *I* had ever touched.

Then she started piling napkins on my lap.

"What are those for?" I asked, as I could not imagine what I would need a bunch of paper napkins for. But she just kept on putting more of them on my lap.

"Those are for the drool," she said.

"What? For the *drool?*"

"It's just in case," she said. "For today, all you'll do is put the device into your mouth and turn it on. The napkins are there just in case you need them."

Now I was really puzzled. The device had lots of buttons and knobs. It was not at all what I had expected.

"This is going to require a learning curve for sure!" I said as we walked through what each little thing did. Then it was almost time to go, so we unhooked the device. I would turn it on the next day after all the required tests were done, and then I would learn to use the device.

They had one last test for me before I left the facility. It was another eye exam.

"Let's look with the refractor," someone said.

Okay, I was totally done. I was tired physically and tired of playing this game, all in the name of science. Yes, I wanted to be helpful. However, I felt that an eye exam with a refractor should have been done first, before all the other tests.

I asked if they had a cup or something and explained that I would be removing my eyes. They got me a contact lenses case, but the prosthetic eyeballs didn't fit in there, so I got a couple of coffee cups, with a paper clip marking the left–side cup. And then out those darned things came. Silence fell in the room, and then the doctor said, "Let's just write NLP, no light perception."

Then, finally, I was escorted out and was able to go get some sleep.

***

Day two.

This was the day I would learn how to hook everything up and what each little button and knob did. I placed the device in my mouth and turned it on. My trainer placed a soft, tubular bar in my hand.

"Hold this in front of you," she said, "and turn the dial up."

She was connected to wi–fi, so she could see everything my

camera could see. I continued to turn up the dial. There was no feeling yet.

"Keep going," she said.

Then there was a tingle. I removed the mouthpiece.

"Did you feel a tingle?" she asked. "Keep turning the device up. There. Now move the bar up and down." I felt a wave across my tongue.

"Stop," she said. Now I could feel a defined line across the middle of my mouth. I was amazed. I moved the foam bar and felt the line move a little. I moved the bar faster, and the line moved faster. I moved it from side to side, stopping in the middle. The wave tingled, with a defined line moving from side to side on my tongue. Then, more gently, I did this again, cross-wise. I felt the device do the same, following whatever I did with the foam bar.

"Totally wild!" I said, as I wiped drool from my face. I had to remove the device to swallow or talk.

Next, we would explore how different items would produce different sensations on my tongue. She would tell me what the items were, and then we would study how each one felt in my mouth. I zoomed in, making the object feel smaller, or zoomed out, making the object feel larger, studying the contrasts, the changes.

That was my second day.

***

Then it was Thursday, the third day, and I found myself getting up at 4:00 a.m. I was enjoying the silence, but I was tired, and wished I could have slept till 7:00 instead of 4:00. It was the strange surroundings, I'm sure.

That day, I would learn about reaching and the depth of an object. There was a table with balls on it.

"Reach out without actually touching anything," she said. "Once you perceive a ball on your tongue, then reach out and touch it on the table."

"Seriously?" I asked. "I can't do that!"

"Let's try it," she said.

So, first finding in my mouth a ball that was on the large table, I reached out for it.

"Now feel how close you are to it!" she said.

I was a mere inch from the object. "Wow!" I gasped. Once again, I had to remove the device to speak, swallow, and wipe drool.

We continued practicing. She placed strips of something on a table, and then I would tell her how many there were and in what directions they were lying. She placed more balls of different sizes on the table, and I would reach out and touch them one by one.

About in the middle of the training, we walked to a hallway. I was to find the door, and I did, in the long, extended hallway. Then we returned to the room we had been working in.

"Mobility will be next," she said. "But first, we're going to play a fun little game using the device. Find the ping pong ball, find the coffee cup, then reach out and drop the ball in the cup without touching the cup."

"Really? I asked. "Surely I can't do that!" I was still wowed by all the information I was gathering in a room merely from sensations on my tongue.

"Let's give it a try, okay?"

Sure enough, I was able to reach out, grab the ball, and drop it in a cup. Several times, then, she moved both the ball and the cup. I would try again, over and over, and each time, I was able to tell the cup from the ball, grab the ball, and drop it in the coffee cup.

Before I did that task, could I have told you what the cup was or what the ball was without my having been informed beforehand what the objects were? No, I couldn't have. But that was the whole purpose of the training, to gradually learn to identify all sorts of objects. The question was, could I be trained to identify the objects around me? Also, how practical would the device be outside the controlled environment?

Each day, I had to recap the task I had learned that day. Gradually, I was mastering the skill of understanding what each object in front of me felt like on my tongue.

On the downside, I was also learning that with each passing day, the amount of drool was increasing. I asked about this, as it was so unpleasant, and it was explained to me that the electrical impulses stimulated the salivary glands. To make things even worse, I was told that it was a side effect that might not subside.

I mentioned to the trainer that I had signed off on a long list of potential side effects, and that excessive, possibly permanent drooling had definitely not been one of them. There had been other pretty alarming potential side effects, though, such as the lack of ability to taste and strange sensations on the tongue. Oh, and death. Let's not forget that one!

She didn't respond, but we continued our training.

Next, I practiced walking down long hallways without my cane. I learned to understand the information to find the elevator, and I mastered reaching out to touch the button to go up or down without having to feel to find it. It was amazing.

I remember walking out to the hallway in the public area and being greeted by many people, who then introduced themselves. There was a huge team involved in setting up this test study in eight facilities across the nation. As I reached out my right hand to shake hands with folks, simultaneously pulling the large mouthpiece from my mouth with my left hand so I could say hello and swallow, I realized that I had drool all over my chest. I was feeling extremely self-conscious by now, and I had to express this to my trainer.

I told her that I loved the number of things I was learning. I was truly excited to walk down a hallway, go through a doorway, and find a chair without the need of my white cane. However, for me, the drool was a major issue. I was already blind, and now I was envisioning myself walking into a public place with a large camera in the middle of my forehead, the glasses, and a large thing in my mouth with cords hanging from it. And drooling.

It was all just too — well, sci–fi–rific was the word that came to me. That is, the device could do terrific, seemingly futuristic things, but given all the drool and the fact that I was unable to speak or swallow with the device in my mouth, I simply had my doubts whether it would really be all that practical for daily life out in the community — or, for that matter, on a public bus.

She listened to all this in silence. At last she asked me, "So, after all the things you've learned to do already, with more to come, are you saying that the drool is a bigger issue then signing a paper informing you that death might occur?"

I paused to think. I had to be honest with her, as well as with myself.

"Well, yes," I said. "I think it might be."

Finally, it was time to return home with the device. For 11 months to come, I was to keep daily records of using it.

Very quickly, however, I learned that the device did not work so well in a non–controlled setting. It was a first-generation device and was not yet approved for general use.

I do hope that all the information gathered from me and the other people in the study will allow the researchers to tweak it a bit, to make it more practical for day–to–day life. Maybe they can make the mouthpiece smaller, so the user can at least swallow with it on, and to lessen the attention that would surely be drawn by such an odd–looking gadget in the first place. And with the drool being added to the whole picture, the original device would surely make for many strange looks when the user entered any kind of eating establishment to seek out a table to dine. It could hardly be an appetizing sight for the other patrons!

So I chose to send the device back, ending my role in what was to have been a year–long study. At home, I was simply unable to master the same skills that I had practiced for a month in the controlled environment.

However, I look forward to any changes and improvements that might be made to this tool, which I sincerely hope will be useful someday as a mobility device, to enhance independence for those of us who are totally without sight. I will be excited to try an updated version of the device.

But next time, the first thing I'll ask about are any drool effects!

Chapter 31

Wrapping Things Up in Closing

I hope you've enjoyed this outline of my journey. Maybe one day I'll write *Cry Purple: The Rest of the Story*. But for now, here are a few closing words.

During the last year and a half of my life on the streets, I was too far gone to even turn tricks to support my addiction. I no longer had any basic survival skills. I no longer sought shelter from the weather and would just sleep outdoors, under trees in parks. I would peer in the windows of the KFC and McDonald's restaurants in the in the area where I existed (I could hardly call it living), and when I spotted food left on tables, I would enter the establishments, pocket the half-eaten food, and dash out again. Or I would dig in the cans outside 7–11 stores. I would crawl into dumpsters to relieve myself. I would beg for change so I could turn on a dryer inside a 24–hour laundromat for some heat.

I was no longer turning tricks, as I was in such bad shape that no one would dare pick me up. People on the set who knew me would sometimes give me a hit of crack just to make me go away.

In short, I was an animal. I prayed for death to find me. No longer able to seek out the safest places to rest my head, I actually sought out the most dangerous ones, just wanting my life, my existence, to end.

I'm not sure exactly *how* I went from hopeless to being with hope. I do know, however, that hope had to come in order for me to be alive and parenting my child today. While still on the streets, I had grown so terribly tired of it all, and eventually, I realized that death was not going to find me. Then, when I was released from prison to that halfway house and I sought a job, it was like a switch had been flipped. Even with some setbacks, as I have already shared, that was the beginning of a better life for me.

Today my prayers are not for death, but of hope and gratitude. Now, to hear the birds singing while I drink my morning coffee is such a far cry from sleeping beside outdoor heating vents, merely smelling coffee from a factory drifting to me on the wind! Now I've learned that no matter what, there can always be a brighter tomorrow.

One of the most freeing moments I had in the early weeks after getting clean was when I was told, "You can't go back and fix the past. However, you can let go of the guilt and shame and move on from this day forward." I embraced that philosophy. Guilt and shame had kept me returning to the crack pipe for decades in order to numb those feelings. But when I learned to let the guilt and shame go at last, I found that I could move forward for the first time in my life.

Letting go doesn't mean that I've forgotten all those experiences. It doesn't mean that I've forgotten those I harmed due to my addiction. It does mean, however, that I now continue doing the right things for the right reasons. So maybe someday, just maybe, I will have a chance to mend some things, to right some wrongs. There is no way that I can ever make up for many, many things that I did, but what I *can* do is do right each day from here on out. That's the best I can do. Maybe it's the best almost anyone can do.

All my life before I went blind, I was sighted and saw the world from the outside in. Today I'm totally blind and can see the world from the inside out. And for me, the view is more beautiful than ever.

Somewhere along the path of struggling to live blind, I found that my blindness had become my blessing. It changed me, changed how I view the world and how the world views me. Is it easy? No. But truly, my new path has been and continues to be a path of growth.

Each challenge I face today is another human experience. I grow through my challenges. They all mold me and shape me, the good ones and the bad ones. Today I embrace hardships and find the joy of triumph whenever I've made it through another one. Each new challenge, each new experience, has something in it for me to take from it. Perhaps I learn that it's something I need to let go of. Perhaps I see that it's something I need to keep in my mind or in my heart, some tool I can use, something that will make me more knowledgeable, better able to cope with whatever experience is going to be the next one to hurtle toward me on the path of life.

My life is a journey. Now I take that journey willingly, moving forward, ever onward, embracing both the good and the bad.

A Special Note from the Author

Thank you for taking the time to read *Cry Purple*. I hope it has given you a different perspective on addiction, homelessness, prostitution, and even blindness. I hope you never see a prostitute, an addict, a felon, or a homeless person in the same way as before.

If you have been moved by this book, please encourage others to read it. If you bought this book from an online buying site, please go there and write a review if you are inspired to do so!

I love to receive comments about my book or personal notes from my readers, so feel free to contact me at **christine.crypurple@gmail.com**

You can visit **www.crypurple.com** or **www.christinesvision.org** to book me for speaking engagements on topics such as overcoming addiction, ex–offender re–entry, homelessness, prostitution/sex trafficking, open adoption, or having a new disability—or just to hear an inspiring, motivational story. I can also share my God story with audiences. In my book, I was careful to not include too much about God's amazing grace in my life; that was to allow those who might be struggling with God to still find hope in my story.

Perhaps your heart was changed by my book. Perhaps what you thought you knew about the life of an addict, a prostitute, or a homeless person was challenged by what I wrote. If so, and if you would like to get involved, then look up organizations and see if you can start making a difference in your own community.

Making a difference can be a simple thing, such as distributing sandwiches with no strings attached or organizing a prayer time just for those on the streets. Help comes in many forms, and doing something is always far better than doing nothing!

As I hinted here and there in the text, there was much that I left out of this book. Besides the obvious fact that no one can tell his or her complete life story in one book, there was a great deal about my early life that I knew various people would not want me to talk about here. So I didn't. But I also left some painful but important events in my more recent life out of the main text. One of those was that after Matt moved out, I tested positive for cancerous cells and had to have a complete hysterectomy. That was a very hard time for me.

Perhaps someday, more about the most difficult parts of my life will go into another book.

I want to make it clear that I did not write this book to bring up old hurts or to re-open closed wounds. I wrote it to allow others to get at least some idea of how hard and painful addiction is, of what depths it can drag you down into. Thus I had no desire to try to pretty anything up. My desire was to come clean at last, to be brutally honest with my reading public. It was important to me to be honest not just about the many bad things that were done to *me* over almost two decades, but also about at least some of the many bad things I did to so many others during all those years when I didn't care how many people I hurt or how many lies I told.

But getting clean is not easy. With the parts of the book that are about the many prejudices and employment difficulties that ex-offenders and ex-addicts face, I wanted to make it as clear as I could that just because you succeed in taking drugs out of the picture, it does not mean that everything magically goes back to normal. There are certainly no magical, fluffy pink clouds to float away on, into a better world. To get to that place, to get to an even *somewhat* better place than the one we were in before, we ex–offenders and ex–addicts have to work very, very hard. So that's what I'm trying to do. As I say in the book, every waking minute of every day, I simply keep trying to do the next right thing.

Now to thank all the many people who helped make this book a reality.

Leonore Dvorkin, of Denver, Colorado, was the main editor of this book. Also, she was the one who came up with the chapter title "Cry Purple," which I then chose as the title of the book.

David Dvorkin, Leonore's husband, did all the technical work required to get the book published. He also designed the cover. I thank both of them for all their time, patience, and tireless efforts to make this project a reality.

Leonore and David offer a diverse range of editing and publishing services. So if you have a book manuscript sitting on a shelf or on your computer, and you'd like some help with making your own dream of being a published author come true, please see their Web page about their services: **http://www.dvorkin.com/ebookpubhelp.html**

The Dvorkins are also prolific writers, with more than 25 published books to their credit. To read about their numerous books, articles, and essays, please visit their websites. Almost all of their books are available as both e–books and paperbacks, and three of them are now in audio format. One of those is Leonore's book about her experience with breast cancer. The title is *Another Chance at Life: A Breast Cancer Survivor's Journey.* You can find that on audible.com.

David's website: **www.dvorkin.com**
Leonore's website: **www.leonoredvorkin.com**

Of course there were also many others involved in this

project. With the whole blind thing and all, I needed much sighted help. So thanks to all the following people. I won't list the individual projects or exactly how you helped, as you all know what you did! On my website, there are more special thanks.

Thanks, guys, for all your love, kindness, and support in this project. God has blessed me with wonderful people in my life. Some have been there but for a moment, and some are there for a lifetime. But for whatever reason, or for whatever length of time, I am thankful for the experience of your presence in my life.

You are:

Christy Bean
Althea and Denny West
Sharon Walker
Jose Lopez
John Kough
Malcolm Garcia
Karen Shoemaker
Sister Birta Sailor/Operation Breakthrough
Kris Judd
Jen and Pat
First Steps for the Blind, KC MO
Reginald (Reggie) George, of Adapt on Demand LLC
Lora McDonald

Some Fellow Authors
and Their Books

All of these authors except Malcolm Garcia are blind, and all are clients of Leonore and David Dvorkin.

I mentioned my good friend **J. Malcolm Garcia**, a reporter and freelance writer, in chapters 19 and 26 of this book. He wrote several articles about me for *The Kansas City Star*, and he has helped me a great deal over the years. You can find his website at **www.malcolmgarcia.com** In addition to the other books listed there, he is the author of a fascinating and very moving autobiographical book called *Riding Through Katrina with the Red Baron's Ghost* (C 2012), available from various online buying sites in both e–book and print formats. Leonore Dvorkin edited that book and also his newest one, *What Wars Leave Behind: The Faceless and the Forgotten* (C 2014, University of Missouri Press).

Brian K. Nash, who has been blind from birth, is a resident of Missouri. Thus far, Brian has written four books for children and two books for teens and adults. Those titles are: *Two Best Friends, Henrietta of Valley View Farm, Midnight to the Rescue, Christmas on Valley View Farm, The Naked Sportsman and Other Stories*, and *Talking with Kids: Everything You've Always Wanted to Know about Blindness*. The first three of his books are charmingly illustrated by Glenda Felbush. All six books are available in both e-book and print formats. For details and buying links, see **www.dvorkin.com/brianknash/**

Patty L. Fletcher, a resident of Tennessee, is the author of an informative and moving book about her intensive training in Morristown, New Jersey in 2011 and her life thereafter with her beloved Seeing Eye dog, Campbell. The title is *Campbell's Rambles: How a Seeing Eye Dog Retrieved My Life* (C 2014). For details, buying links, photos of the author and her dog, and much more, please see **www.dvorkin.com/pattyfletcher/** (Note: THE SEEING EYE and SEEING EYE are registered trademarks of The Seeing Eye, Inc.)

Robert T. (Bob) Branco, a resident of Massachusetts, is the publisher of *The Consumer Vision Magazine*: **www.consumervisionmagazine.com** He also wrote many articles for the *Matilda Ziegler Magazine for the Blind,* which has now ceased publication. He is the author of several books: *What We Love to Eat* (C 2012), a cookbook made up of recipes that were all submitted by blind contributors; *As I See It: From a Blind Man's Perspective* — Revised and Expanded Edition (C 2013); *My Home Away from Home: Life at Perkins School for the Blind* (C 2013); and *Weighing Things Up: Essays on Trends, Technology, and Present-Day Society* (C 2014). For details and buying links, see **www.dvorkin.com/robertbranco/**

Howard A. Geltman, a resident of Connecticut, is the author of an autobiographical book about his childhood and teen years at Oak Hill School for the Blind, in Hartford, Connecticut. The title is *A Few Moments in Time* (C 2011). The striking photograph used for the cover of Howard's book was taken by another blind student at the school. For details and buying links, see **www.dvorkin.com/howardgeltman/**

81928193R00133

Made in the USA
Columbia, SC
27 November 2017